The
fasting
EDGE
JOURNAL

The
fasting
EDGE
JOURNAL

Jentezen Franklin

CHARISMA
HOUSE

Most CHARISMA HOUSE BOOK GROUP products are available at special quantity discounts for bulk purchase for sales promotions, premiums, fund-raising, and educational needs. For details, write Charisma House Book Group, 600 Rinehart Road, Lake Mary, Florida 32746, or telephone (407) 333-0600.

THE FASTING EDGE JOURNAL by Jentezen Franklin
Published by Charisma House
Charisma Media/Charisma House Book Group
600 Rinehart Road
Lake Mary, Florida 32746
www.charismahouse.com

Unless otherwise noted, all Scripture quotations are from the New King James Version of the Bible. Copyright © 1979, 1980, 1982 by Thomas Nelson, Inc., publishers. Used by permission.

Scripture quotations marked AMP are from the Amplified Bible. Old Testament copyright © 1965, 1987 by the Zondervan Corporation. The Amplified New Testament copyright © 1954, 1958, 1987 by the Lockman Foundation. Used by permission.

Scripture quotations marked NAS are from the New American Standard Bible, Copyright © 1960, 1962, 1963, 1968, 1971, 1972, 1973, 1975, 1977, 1995 by The Lockman Foundation. Used by permission. (www.Lockman.org)

Scripture quotations marked NIV are from the Holy Bible, New International Version. Copyright © 1973, 1978, 1984, International Bible Society. Used by permission.

Cover design by Justin Evans
Design Director: Bill Johnson

Visit the author's website at www.jentezenfranklin.org.

Library of Congress Cataloging-in-Publication Data

Franklin, Jentezen, 1962-
The fasting edge journal / Jentezen Franklin.
pages cm
Companion volume to: The fasting edge.
ISBN 978-1-61638-850-8
1. Fasting--Religious aspects--Christianity. 2. Christianity. 3. Spiritual journals.
I. Franklin, Jentezen, 1962- Fasting edge. II. Title.

BV5055.F7323 2012
248.4'7--dc23

                  2011048169

E-book ISBN: 978-1-61638-857-7

12 13 14 15 16 — 9 8 7 6 5 4 3
Printed in the United States of America

Is this not the fast that I have chosen:
To loose the bonds of wickedness,
To undo the heavy burdens,
To let the oppressed go free,
And that you break every yoke?
Is it not to share your bread with the hungry,
And that you bring to your house the poor who are
    cast out;
When you see the naked, that you cover him,
And not hide yourself from your own flesh?
Then your light shall break forth like the morning,
Your healing shall spring forth speedily,
And your righteousness shall go before you;
The glory of the LORD *shall be your rear guard.*
Then you shall call, and the LORD *will answer;*
You shall cry, and He will say, "Here I am."

If you take away the yoke from your midst,
The pointing of the finger, and speaking wickedness,
If you extend your soul to the hungry
And satisfy the afflicted soul,
Then your light shall dawn in the darkness,
And your darkness shall be as the noonday.
The LORD *will guide you continually,*
And satisfy your soul in drought,
And strengthen your bones;
You shall be like a watered garden,
And like a spring of water, whose waters do not fail.

*—*ISAIAH 58:6–11

CONTENTS

I am so glad you have chosen to let fasting accomplish its many purposes in your life. You know, every believer loses the edge in his or her life from time to time, including me. In my own life I've learned that it's vital to take the time to fast and pray to interrupt the dulling effects of everyday life and ministry. Anytime I feel myself getting dull spiritually, I fast. It may be a short fast or a longer one, but I have learned that fasting releases much more in my life than I can even comprehend. Fasting is a way to sharpen my edge and prepare the way for God to accomplish so much more through His Spirit working in my life than I could ever accomplish in my own limited strength. Whether I fast privately or corporately, it allows me to regain the cutting edge of the anointing of the Holy Spirit in my life.

Perhaps at one time you sensed the anointing of the Lord on your life, and you were going for it. You had the edge. Your life was consecrated to God, and you had a deep passion for spiritual things. But something shifted. These days you feel like you've lost the edge. What's worse is that the enemy has convinced you that it is out of sight, out of reach, and you can never reclaim it.

Have you bought the lie that your anointing, your purpose, your dream, your family, your lost children—these are all gone forever? Given the economic downturn this nation has experienced over the past several years, many have faced dire circumstances, having lost jobs, lost homes and cars, lost respect, and lost all hope. But I want to encourage you today that God can give you your edge back—and fasting is the way to bring it about.

If you are tired of dull church, if you are tired of a cold, dry, barren relationship with Jesus, it is time to regain your edge. It is time to declare a spiritual fast. The Bible declares that:

The steps of a good man are ordered by the LORD,
And He delights in his way.

—PSALM 37:23

As you set aside this time to focus on God and His Word, I believe God is going to establish who He is in your life again, afresh and anew. I believe God will give you guidance and bless you to do mighty things.

Your life takes on a powerful edge when you fast. As you use this fasting and prayer devotional over the next twenty-one days, I challenge you to press into God and expect greater passion, purpose, and joy in His presence than you've ever known before.

The short answer to this question is that fasting draws us closer to God. That might sound simplistic, but it's not. Drawing closer to God through fasting and prayer will release His supernatural power in ways that will affect your future, your family, and every aspect of your life.

I like to say that fasting is a short-term investment that releases long-term rewards. It is like taking the time to sharpen your ax before cutting down a tree. Sure, you can keep cutting with a dull ax, powering along in your own strength, but I would rather get more done operating under the power of God! When you set aside time for fasting and prayer, you see greater results. Just as sharpening an ax puts the edge back, fasting gives you back your edge. It gives you the power to do far more than you could possibly accomplish in your own strength and finite understanding.

There are three simple but important things you need to do before you start fasting to regain your edge. First, make up your mind that you *are* going to regain your edge. There is power in a made-up mind. You must choose to change the direction you've been going. You must decide to reject the status quo in your walk with God. You must decide that He is bigger than the problems you might be facing in this moment. Now is the time to make up your mind that you will believe Him for what seems to be impossible and stop believing the lies of the enemy who wants to see you defeated. Make up your mind that you are going to get your edge back.

The second thing you must do to regain your edge is to confess that you have lost it. This might seem like a given, but you'd be surprised how many Christians are walking around in denial about their situation. Going through religious motions day after day has dulled their spiritual senses and blinded them to their own condition. This is no way to live. It is not what God has called you to do. If you have lost your passion, if you have lost your edge, if your joy is gone and your dreams have died, be swift to confess it to your Father God right now. You may even want to confess it to someone who can pray with you and help you find your way back.

The third thing you need to do is take action. God will not do for you what you can do for yourself. God intends for you to do your part in regaining the edge. When you declare a fast and set aside time for prayer, you are taking the first step in gaining the sharp edge that God has provided for you to be effective. Be sure to write down your specific reasons for fasting, what you plan to give up during your fast, the date you plan to start, and the date you plan to end. Putting all of these things in writing will help you stay the course until you've completed your time of fasting. I've provided a page following the Preparation section of this book where you can write these things down.

Each daily entry of this twenty-one-day fasting journal provides you with an excerpt from my book *The Fasting Edge*, along with a suggested daily prayer focus, scripture, questions to take your thoughts deeper, and some practical tips to help you be successful in your fast.

You've picked up this journal because you have decided to regain your edge through fasting. As you do your part, I'm in agreement that sharp ideas are going to come to you. Sharp relationships with new people are going to add significantly to your life. Cutting-edge creativity is going to flow your way as you begin to hunger and thirst for more. Get ready to begin your fast!

LEARN FROM GREAT MEN AND WOMEN OF THE BIBLE WHO EXPERIENCED THE POWER OF FASTING.

What is your greatest need today? Do you need wisdom, power, healing, or protection? The Bible tells of men and women with the same struggles that you face today. They sought God's face through prayer and fasting for the different seasons of their lives, and so can you.

1. The disciples' fast

The disciples' fast is a fast that frees you from addictions to sin or besetting sins as referred to in Hebrews 12:1. Besetting sins are those that ensnare us and hinder us from achieving God's purpose for our lives.

In Mark, chapter 9, Christ's disciples were frustrated because they could not cast out an evil spirit. Jesus said, "This kind can come out by nothing but prayer and fasting" (v. 29). Through fasting we can break free from the addictions and habits that are not pleasing to God.

Lisa from Georgia wrote to me, "I overcame a lifetime of smoking and am seventeen months free from nicotine addiction." Suzan from Florida sent this praise report: "I fasted in January for my mother to be delivered from an addiction to alcohol. She is now free from the desire for alcohol…with no physical withdrawal symptoms. This is a miracle. Praise God!"

2. The Ezra fast

The Ezra fast is found in Ezra 8:21. Ezra had been given silver and gold to take back to Jerusalem from King Artaxerxes (Ezra 7:14–17). But there was a problem—thieves!

Maybe you feel like thieves have stolen what belongs to you financially. When Ezra faced an uncertain financial journey, what did he do? He declared a fast, and God answered his prayer! If you will fast, pray, and obey God's commandments, God said you would be blessed (Deut. 28:2).

3. The Samuel fast

When the Philistines were preparing to attack Israel, Samuel declared a fast for national revival. Samuel told the people to fast and seek God to return His presence to the nation (1 Sam. 7:3).

Our society today critically needs believers who will take the Samuel fast—a fast for national revival.

> If My people who are called by My name will humble themselves, and pray and seek My face, and turn from their wicked ways, then I will hear from heaven, and will forgive their sin and heal their land.
>
> —2 CHRONICLES 7:14

We can return God's presence and glory to our personal lives and our nation if we fast, pray, and seek Him now.

4. The Elijah fast

One of the most powerful fasts is the Elijah fast. It breaks negative emotional feelings and habits. When Jezebel sent word that she wanted to kill Elijah, he became so distraught that he was an emotional wreck (1 Kings 19:4). He was depressed, even suicidal.

That's when an angel came to Elijah and instructed him to journey back into the presence of God. The Bible says that Elijah fasted for forty days and forty nights as he returned to Horeb, the mountain of God. God delivered Elijah from feelings of suicide and fear. He gave him hope, courage, and direction. Whether you suffer from emotional bad habits, a negative self-image, fear, insecurities, depression, or some other emotional bondage, fasting will help open your heart and mind to hear the still, small voice of God.

5. The widow's fast

The widow's fast is about meeting the humanitarian needs of other people while you are fasting. In 1 Kings 17:10–16, we read the vivid story about a woman with very little who helped the man of God, Elijah. It was all part of God's plan.

The widow made a choice to fast so that someone else could eat. The Book of Isaiah puts it this way: "Is not the fast I have chosen…is it not to share your bread with the hungry, and that you bring to your house the poor who are cast out?" (Isa. 58:6–7).

Today, you can meet the humanitarian needs of other people while you're fasting by using the money you would normally feed yourself with to help a food bank, support world missions, or give to some other ministry that is helping the needy. When you do that, it pleases God and He will meet your needs. In the story of the widow, God multiplied the meal in her barrel to last for *three and a half years*!

6. The Paul fast

Are you faced with a major life decision and don't know what to do? Maybe you have a job opportunity, a broken relationship, or an unfulfilled dream. God has provided a way you can discern His voice—the Paul fast. Saul was going the wrong way in life. He was hunting down followers of Christ and persecuting them when the light of God's truth knocked him off his path (Acts 9:3–6).

Saul headed to Damascus and "was three days without sight, and neither ate nor drank" (v. 9). Saul didn't know what to do. But he fasted for God's divine direction. Then God sent the disciple Ananias to Saul with guidance (v. 17). Through this process Saul became Paul, one of God's chosen disciples. Through his fast Paul got the direction he needed, and so can you.

Angela from Arkansas needed a job when she began her fast. "I was believing God for a new job. I received a call from the CEO of a company offering me a full-time position with a salary increase and benefits. I thank God! Fasting really works!"

7. The Daniel fast

The Daniel fast is a partial and prolonged fast that yields health and healing. Found in Daniel chapter 10, the Daniel fast is a fast from meats, sweets, breads, and any drink but water for twenty-one days (Dan. 10:2–3).

Another time, Daniel and three others refused to eat the king's meat, and they "appeared better and fatter in flesh than all the young men who ate the portion of the king's delicacies" (Dan. 1:15). Daniel and his men were healthier!

8. The John the Baptist fast

John and his disciples fasted often, according to Matthew 9:14. He was on the Nazirite diet, which fasted alcohol all the time. He ate little more than locusts and wild honey (Matt. 3:1–4). Because of John the Baptist's constant fasting, I believe he had a greater testimony and influence on the lives of people in his generation than any other man (Matt. 11:1; John 1:6–7).

Jodi of Lousiana wrote, "I chose to join in the twenty-one-day fast. For many years I have been praying for [my sister's] marriage and her salvation.

She gave her heart to the Lord Jesus Christ on the twenty-first day of the fast! What a super release of His favor!"

Maria from the Philippines said that by the third week of her fast she had received invitations to teach outside of her church. "It was like what you said about God just opening doors for ministry. Fasting now is a way of life I cannot do without."

9. The Esther fast

The Esther fast is the fast for protection against danger. We live in a world full of predators, disasters, and evil. But don't live in fear. God has provided the blessing of protection.

Esther was in a very dangerous position. Her cousin Mordecai discovered a plot by Haman, one of the king's advisors, to destroy her family. When he asked for Esther's help, she knew it was very dangerous to approach the king without being called for. She could lose her life. So Esther declared a three-day fast for God's protection (Esther 4:16).

Haman wanted to hang Mordecai on the gallows he was building in his courtyard, but God turned it around and the evil conspirator was hanged instead—on his own gallows! When you fast and pray, God will extend His protection to you and your household.

REASONS TO FAST RECAP

- THE DISCIPLES' FAST—for freedom from addictions to sin

- THE EZRA FAST—for help with financial troubles

- THE SAMUEL FAST—for national revival

- THE ELIJAH FAST—for negative emotional feelings and habits

- THE WIDOW'S FAST—for humanitarian needs of others

- THE PAUL FAST—for major life decisions

- THE DANIEL FAST—for health and healing

- THE JOHN THE BAPTIST FAST—for influence on others

- THE ESTHER FAST—for protection against danger

A s you prepare for this incredible twenty-one-day journey of fasting and prayer, there are a few things I want to impart to you. If you've read my book *Fasting* and used its companion *Fasting Journal*, these steps may sound familiar. I've repeated them in this journal because I believe it's important to follow these practical guidelines *every* time you prepare to fast.

If you do not already have one, establish a place and time where you can pray. Prayer is critical during the fast to break through and hear what the Lord is saying to you. Use this journal to keep track of your journey. You will rejoice years from now to see what amazing things have come to pass.

How do you determine what type of fast you will do for the twenty-one days? That is between you and God, and it should be a matter of prayer before you begin. You may feel led to go on a full fast in which you only drink liquids for a certain number of days—especially plenty of water. On that type of fast, you may also take in clear broth and 100 percent juices in order to maintain your strength.

Of the many different fasts mentioned in Scripture, another commonly practiced fast is the partial fast. A partial fast can be interpreted many ways. It usually involves giving up particular foods and drink for an extended period of time. The most frequently used example of a partial fast is found in the Book of Daniel, chapters 1 and 10. In the beginning of his captivity in Babylon (Dan. 1), Daniel and three companions refused to eat the choice meats and sweets from the king's table, asking instead to have only vegetables and water. They did this for ten days to prove they would be just as healthy as the king's men.

The partial fast is ideal for people with health conditions that would prevent them from participating in other types of fasts. If you have a health condition, talk to your doctor before you start fasting and create a plan to abstain from certain foods without adversely affecting your health. (You may even discover that partial fasting improves your health because of the elimination of unhealthy foods and beverages.)

Although you will be abstaining from food as your sacrifice, do not let the legalistic aspects of a fast crowd out the relational aspects of closeness with the Lord. He knows your heart. Closeness with the Lord is your goal, and fasting is the method to reach your goal.

There are a few other things to focus on during this time that will help you maintain a "clean vessel." For example, you should refrain from critical speaking, spreading negative words about or to anyone else. Our church practices this discipline each year, and the results are amazing. Consider limiting how much you watch TV and how much time you spend on things that are distracting. Your fast will be not only a season of sacrifice but also a season of increased warfare. You need to be at your best.

And, of course, you will enjoy many spiritual rewards of fasting, like hearing the voice of God more clearly. I love those times when it's just Jesus and me and the tears begin to flow. My favorite time is when He seems to step into the room and I am overwhelmed. I call these "sweet spots."

It is also important to have your favorite worship music available and to spend time worshiping often. And, if possible, I highly recommend establishing some form of accountability during the fast, either with someone who is fasting with you or a prayer partner.

In Daniel chapter 10, Daniel was grieved and burdened with the revelation he'd received for Israel. He ate no choice breads or meats and drank no wine for three weeks. Then he described the angel who was sent to him—but had been delayed by the prince of Persia for twenty-one days—with the answers Daniel sought. His fast broke the power of the delayer and released the angels of God so that God's purposes could be revealed and served.

Whenever you begin a fast, remember, if it doesn't mean anything to you, it won't mean anything to God. Without being combined with prayer and the Word, fasting is little more than dieting. But I want you to realize something very important: Fasting itself is a continual prayer before God. There may be days when heaven opens and your heart is prompted to deep times of prayer. But there may be other days when your energy is sapped and you just cannot seem to focus in prayer at all. Don't condemn yourself. God sees your sacrifice.

I commit to fast from (date) _____ to (date) _____

The reason I am fasting:

_____

_____

_____

_____

What am I fasting from?

_____

_____

_____

_____

The results of my fast:

_____

_____

_____

_____

Do you remember the passion you had for the Lord when you were first saved? Do you remember what it was like during those first few weeks after Jesus lifted the heavy burden of sin from your life and made you clean and new? When you have that kind of passion, it is transferred to your family. Passion is transferable, but lack of passion is also transferable. The people around you notice a difference, and your passion stirs passion in their lives. However, if you have lost the edge, lost your passion, then the lack of passion is transferred. This is especially true for worship leaders, pastors, and church leaders.

We all need godly mentors in our lives, men and women of God who know how to reach out and touch heaven; a proven brother or sister who can come alongside us, hear our mistakes, and speak life and grace to help restore us. As Paul instructed the Galatian church:

> Brethren, if a man is overtaken in any trespass, you who are spiritual restore such a one in a spirit of gentleness, considering yourself lest you also be tempted. Bear one another's burdens, and so fulfill the law of Christ. For if anyone thinks himself to be something, when he is nothing, he deceives himself.
>
> —GALATIANS 6:1–3

Where did you lose it? Was it due to life's battering and disappointments suffered along the way? Though it may not seem so now, your present difficulty may be instrumental to your future happiness.

Let today's circumstances drive you to your knees in a season of prayer and fasting. Go back to the place where the edge was lost. Was it through sin that you need to confess? Go back to that place and get it under the blood of Jesus. The altar is not just for those coming to the Lord for the first time. The altar is a place to get free from that thing that weighs you down and drowns out your fiery passion for God. Alterations are made at the altar. The altar is a place to *alter* your direction and get back on the right track with God.

When you allow the cross of Calvary to touch your life afresh, when you come to the foot of the cross and confess your sin, it changes everything. Suddenly the supernatural possibilities become much more natural!

> God still plans to raise up men and women in this generation who have the edge, the power of the Holy Spirit operating in their lives.

On your first day of fasting, remember:

- Read your Bible and spend time in prayer.

- Make sure you drink enough water.

- Expect headaches; hunger pangs; and cravings for food, sugar, and caffeine.

Thoughts for your journal:

- When did your prayer life and worship grow dull?

- Can you identify what caused you to lose your edge?

_____

_____

_____

PRAYER FOCUS DAY 1: Renewed Passion

There's nothing Satan loves more than a passionless Christian. In Matthew 5:13 Jesus compares this spiritual condition to salt that has lost its flavor. It has become ineffective and no longer serves a purpose. It's time to ask God to bring back your passion and purpose. As you begin your fast, determine in your heart that you won't be the same person coming out of this fast as you are going into it. Don't live another day of dull, ineffective Christianity. Pray that over the course of these twenty-one days God will give you a new passion, a renewing of your first love, of the days when all you wanted to do was read His Word and spend time praying and worshiping Him. Pray that the fire in your heart will burn for the things that matter to His heart: showing lost souls the way home, dispelling the works of darkness, and advancing His kingdom.

What is God revealing to you as you seek Him for renewed passion?

_____

_____

_____

_____

_____

_____

> I know you are enduring patiently and are bearing up for My name's sake, and you have not fainted or become exhausted or grown weary. But I have this [one charge to make] against you: that you have left (abandoned) the love that you had at first [you have deserted Me, your first love]....Repent (change the inner man to meet God's will) and do the works you did previously [when first you knew the Lord].
>
> —REVELATION 2:3–5, AMP

DAY 2: Take Out the Trash

If you have lost your edge because of sin, it is time to get alone with God. Fasting and prayer can help you sever addictions to tobacco, to drugs, to alcohol, to pornography. Fasting and prayer help you cut out the double life, the secret sins that you believe are hidden from everyone else—but they are not hidden to God. Sin will clog the pipeline of all future blessings. Fasting is the spiritual "Drano" that unclogs the flow of the living water in your soul.

Fasting makes you sensitive to the "trash" that tries to invade your life. We don't have any movie channels on our TV because so much of it is just filth. But I was flipping through the channels one evening and was shocked to find about five movie channels available. I couldn't believe what I was seeing in my home! We called the cable company to find out what was going on. I wasn't paying for that and did not want my children stumbling across it either. The cable company explained that it was a free sixty-day trial! In other words, they pipe that stuff in unsolicited to get people hooked. Needless to say we had it taken off immediately.

You may think that is insignificant, but remember, the enemy is prowling. He is sneaking around. You hear a twig snap behind you and convince yourself that it is no big deal...but he is about to pounce. I remember the old folks saying, "The devil is in the details." What you feed your mind matters. The kind of music you feed your soul matters. Fasting doesn't just pertain to what you put in your stomach, but what you feed your soul and spirit as well.

> Do you not know that your body is the temple of the Holy Spirit who is in you, whom you have from God, and you are not your own? For you were bought at a price; therefore glorify God in your body and in your spirit, which are God's.
>
> —1 Corinthians 6:19–20

Seasons of fasting and prayer help you get your sensitivity back to the things of God. When you have become dull by the constant bombardment of trash all around you, fasting helps you get the edge back to cut through the trash and clean it out. The anointing of God is precious and should not be handled as a light thing. When we begin a twenty-one-day fast at the first of the year, one of the things we always focus on is getting the trash out of the temple.

Cry out to God as you fast and pray. Invite God to begin a demolition in your life. He's going to tear down who you used to be as He raises you up to become who you were meant to be, who you were born to be!

> God had something in mind when He put you on this earth. And I want to challenge you to whatever degree you can to fulfill every part of His purpose.

On your second day of fasting, remember:

- Read your Bible and spend time in prayer.

- Make sure you get enough rest.

- Expect the second and third days to be the hardest.

Thoughts for your journal:

- What areas of sinfulness in your life is God revealing to you?

- In addition to prayer, what practical steps can you take to gain victory over this sin?

_____

_____

_____

PRAYER FOCUS DAY 2: Cleansing From Sin

As you pray today, examine your heart. Ask the Lord to shine His light into every dark hidden corner and reveal the things you've been holding back and unwilling to deal with until now. Allow His perfect love to cast out all fear as you bring these things before Him today and ask for forgiveness. It's time to take this next step so you can leave the old life behind and regain your edge. Read the entire chapter of Psalm 51 in conjunction with your prayer time today. David wrote this psalm after having an affair with Bathsheba and plotting the death of her husband. May it encourage you that there is nothing God can't forgive; there's no sin too great for His mercy and grace to cover. True freedom is waiting for you once you confess everything and ask Him to remove it from your life. Hold nothing back. He wants to take it all and replace it with His forgiveness, healing, and unconditional love.

Write your confession to God and accept His forgiveness:

_____

_____

_____

_____

_____

_____

> Create in me a clean heart, O God, and renew a steadfast spirit within me. Do not cast me away from Your presence, and do not take Your Holy Spirit from me. Restore to me the joy of Your salvation, and uphold me by Your generous Spirit.
>
> —PSALM 51:10–12

When you get right down to it, only two things determine your destiny: your *choices* and your *responses* to God. The Word of God is full of choices. The entire twenty-eighth chapter of Deuteronomy is dedicated to choosing to do right and be blessed or to do wrong and be cursed. Moses's successor, Joshua, called upon the people of Israel to make up their minds. He gave them a simple choice:

> If serving the LORD seems undesirable to you, then choose for yourselves this day whom you will serve, whether the gods your ancestors served beyond the River, or the gods of the Amorites, in whose land you are living. But as for me and my household, we will serve the LORD.
>
> —JOSHUA 24:15, NIV

The underlying theme of this choice can be summed up in the words of Romans 12:9, where Paul instructs believers, "Abhor what is evil. Cling to what is good."

I remember when I was twelve and could not wait to turn thirteen and become an official "teenager." When you are growing up, time just drags on so slowly. When I was fifteen, I could not wait to turn sixteen and start driving. The next two years seemed to take an eternity to pass by, but finally my eighteenth birthday arrived. But suddenly time sped up. Before I knew it, I was twenty-five, then thirty, forty, and at the writing of this book, nearly fifty! Decades passed by in a blur. Looking back, I am grateful for godly parents who helped me understand how to make right decisions early on in life. I look at my wife and children whom I love; I look at the ministry where God has placed me and the influence He has given, and I know that on my own I am not qualified enough, not gifted enough, not educated enough to be doing what I am doing. Then again, it is not our gifts and education that set the course for our lives, but our choices and our responses to God.

The Lord touched my heart in a service when I was thirteen years old, and I remember making the decision that very night that I would be a virgin when I got married. I remember thinking it through and planning how I would avoid temptation in order to stick to that decision. I can still remember the day that I made up my mind that I would never touch alcohol again, that I would never touch cigarettes again. Those were not popular decisions!

They were decisions that took me off the broad path where most of my friends walked, setting my course instead on the narrow path. Whenever you make a choice *against* one thing—you make a choice *for* something else.

When you make up your mind to abhor evil, you make the choice to cling to what is good. In the same manner, when you choose to ignore the prompting of the Lord in an area, you are making a choice to do something that opposes His best plan for your life.

When you choose to do what is right, you influence others. When you choose to fast and pray, your children learn to fast and pray. When you choose to abhor evil and cleave to good, your children, your friends, and your family will learn to do so too.

> Choosing to do right is not always easy, but God's grace is sufficient to see you through.

On your third day of fasting, remember:

- Read your Bible and spend time in prayer.

- Expect this day to be one of the hardest as your body adjusts to the change in eating habits.

- Turn off the television and other distractions.

Thoughts for your journal:

- Are you wavering in your decision to do right, or maybe even your decision to fast?

- Can you think of ways to encourage yourself and stick to your choices?

_____

_____

_____

PRAYER FOCUS DAY 3: Resisting Temptation

Temptations—all of us face them. Even seasoned believers can make wrong choices in moments of weakness. We've all seen Christians who devote their entire lives to God, building ministries or personal legacies, only to watch them fall to pieces when some secret sin or scandal is exposed. Unfortunately, one wrong choice can overshadow a lifetime of service to the King. They ran the race but faltered just before the finish line. I'm not saying God can't forgive and restore. He certainly does. But let's choose today to finish well. Let's choose to stay the course and not get sidelined by temptations. This is one of the reasons why fasting is so important. It sharpens your sensitivity to areas where you are allowing yourself to drift too close to the line—or even over the line and into sinfulness. Your choices affect your destiny. Choose today to do right, no matter what it takes, and pray for the strength and endurance to finish well.

Write a plan for how you will respond in moments of temptation:

_____

_____

_____

_____

> Therefore submit to God. Resist the devil and he will flee from you.
>
> —JAMES 4:7

Hard times are unavoidable. They are going to come, whether you have made up your mind how you will respond or not. If you have not already made up your mind to honor God no matter the consequences, then you will most likely compromise. That's why the Bible says:

> Remember now your Creator in the days of your youth, *before the difficult days come.*
> —ECCLESIASTES 12:1, EMPHASIS ADDED

There will come a day when your responses to God and the choices you have made will be tested. That day came for Job. Satan came to test him to the core. In one single day Job lost everything that he cared about and loved. His children, his servants, his herds, his properties…all destroyed in the blink of an eye. Throughout the day that faithful man of God was pummeled with one tragic story of loss and destruction following immediately on the heels of another. The final blow came in the news that all ten of his children, who were dining together at the home of his eldest son, had been killed when a windstorm destroyed the house. Hearing that news:

> Job arose and tore his robe and shaved his head, and he fell to the ground and worshiped. And he said: "Naked I came from my mother's womb, and naked shall I return there. The LORD gave, and the LORD has taken away; blessed be the name of the LORD." In all this Job did not sin nor charge God with wrong.
> —JOB 1:20–22

That amazes me. I cannot imagine how my heart would break if something happened to just one of my children. Job immediately demonstrated the outward signs of mourning in that culture, but the powerful thing was what he demonstrated from the inside: he fell to the ground…*and worshiped.* In the face of utter calamity and loss, his heart was already prepared to worship God no matter what. Even our brokenness and great pain can be poured out on the feet of Jesus as an offering of worship.

What was Job's secret? Years before he had made up his mind. Back when he had his good health, when he was raising his children and watching his blessings increase, back before the testing came—he made up his mind how he would respond to God. When all was lost and his body was saying, "Give up"…when his circumstances were saying, "Throw in the towel and quit!"…when his neighbors were asking, "Where are all your kids, Job? Where are all your flocks and great wealth?"…when his wife said, "Curse God and die"…Job had endurance for the trial. He was conditioned for the marathon.

When Job was younger and stronger, he responded to his Redeemer and made right choices that prepared him for the hard times so that he would not waiver in the face of such utter loss. He made up his mind that no matter what, he would praise his God.

> There always comes a day of
> testing. That is when the value of
> a made-up mind truly counts.

On your fourth day of fasting, remember:

- Listen as you pray.

- Record what God is saying to you as you fast.

- Your body should feel more adjusted to the fast today.

Thoughts for your journal:

- What are some hard times you've already experienced, and how did you respond?

- How do you think fasting and prayer will prepare you to handle hard times ahead?

_____

_____

_____

PRAYER FOCUS DAY 4: A Worship-Filled Heart

As you spend time fasting and praying today, your spirit is being strengthened and prepared to respond with a heart of worship in the difficult times and battles that lie ahead. All of us go through scenarios in life that we never could have planned or dreamed up. In my life there have been times where everything worked perfectly and other times when it seemed that nothing was going right. The key is to learn to worship, to humble yourself with fasting and prayer, and to seek God's face no matter the transition. Without spending time waiting on God when the skies are cloudless, you might find yourself completely unprepared to handle the storms of life. Paul said he had learned how to be content no matter the circumstances. That is a goal we should all pray for and strive for. When you spend time in fasting and prayer, you become rooted and grounded in your faith, ready to weather any storm. Even when crisis comes, when you fast and pray and seek God's face, you can receive wisdom, plans, and resources to endure and overcome.

Describe some stormy circumstances that you need to respond to with worship:

_____

_____

_____

_____

> For I have learned in whatever state I am, to be content: I know how to be abased, and I know how to abound. Everywhere and in all things I have learned both to be full and to be hungry, both to abound and to suffer need. I can do all things through Christ who strengthens me.
>
> —PHILIPPIANS 4:11–13

Whether you call it your purpose, your calling, or your destiny, God has a specific plan for your life, one that your choices and responses to Him will unlock. There is a list of ordinary people in the eleventh chapter of the Book of Hebrews. Though ordinary, they did extraordinary things for God because of their choices and responses to God. They never lost the vision, and in the worst of times they refused to turn back.

When Abraham decided to leave home and follow God, he had no idea where that journey would take him—most likely, neither will you. When you follow God, not everybody will go with you. Your dream could be their nightmare. Go with God when He is calling you out of your comfort zone. If failure is not a possibility, then success doesn't mean anything.

When you start taking some risks, you will pray like you have never prayed before, and you will fast like never before because your life depends on it! Make up your mind to finish this fast, and God will give you the grace to complete it. The moment you decide that you've come too far with God on this fast to turn back, you'll begin to see His hand at work in your life.

Make up your mind that you will not be one who compromises when things get tough. Begin to make fasting and prayer a regular part of your lifestyle to develop the confidence and endurance you need to succeed.

God can do more in one moment than you or I can do in a lifetime. Things that would take years in the natural, God can do in a flash. I truly believe that fasting often accelerates your destiny. In other words, it gets you there faster!

I am convinced that God accelerated this ministry ten years ahead of what it would have been without the days of fasting and prayer that were sown. Fasting got me here faster. I've seen it happen over and over in my life. I was given opportunities that pastors who had been in ministry many years longer than myself had not yet been given. When Free Chapel built the building we currently occupy, we were here only five years before paying it off and becoming completely debt free. Our California campus grew from a few hundred attendees to a few thousand in just a couple of years.

Again and again I believe God has accelerated my destiny because of fasting. I wholeheartedly believe He desires and is able to do the same for you.

> Make up your mind to go after God with all your heart. Set aside regular times of fasting and prayer, seeking to know Him better.

On your fifth day of fasting, remember:

- Journal your journey and the things God is revealing to you about your destiny.

- Headaches and cravings should be subsiding today.

- Try chewing on a clove, mint leaf, or sprig of parsley to help avoid bad breath as your body detoxifies.

Thoughts for your journal:

- Is there an area of your life where you believe you've been following God's direction, but it hasn't gone the way you thought?

- How do you want to see God move on your behalf in this area?

_____

_____

_____

_____

PRAYER FOCUS DAY 5: Clearer Direction

Do you want to know God's direction for the next phase of your life? Ask Him. During this fast pray and ask God to define His plans and direction for your life. Pray for dreams, visions, and other forms of divine guidance. Vision comes from God to help His people establish His kingdom on the earth. Have you been distracted from fulfilling things you felt God has called you to do in the past? How has this fast helped you to refocus on that calling or destiny? Never settle for less than God's best for your life. Allow this fast to help you refocus on the destiny God has planned for you.

Write down your destiny, and focus on it during your fast:

_____

_____

> Write the vision and make it plain on
> tablets…though it tarries, wait for it.
>
> —HABAKKUK 2:2–3

Have you ever wondered why Jesus fasted? Jesus is called the Son of Man and the Son of God. He was all man and all God in one form. But even though He was God's Son and He and the Father were "one," we also know that before Jesus began His earthly ministry, He was led by the Holy Spirit into the desert on a forty-day fast.

> When He had been baptized, Jesus came up immediately from the water; and behold, the heavens were opened to Him, and He saw the Spirit of God descending like a dove and alighting upon Him. And suddenly a voice came from heaven, saying, "This is My beloved Son, in whom I am well pleased." Then Jesus was led up by the Spirit into the wilderness to be tempted by the devil. And when He had fasted forty days and forty nights, afterward He was hungry.
>
> —MATTHEW 3:16–4:2

With the water of the Jordan River still running down His face and clothes, God's voice was heard declaring Jesus to be His Son, in whom He was well pleased. What better time to launch a public ministry than when God Himself publicly proclaims His pleasure in you! That is how man typically chooses to do things—in his own strength. But instead of having crowds of devoted followers clamoring about, Jesus went into total isolation for forty days and nights, eating nothing and being tempted by the devil the entire time.

I wonder if Jesus would have succeeded over the enemy in that wilderness if He had not fasted. The Bible does not detail the temptations Jesus endured during the fast, only those that came at the end of it. I would imagine most of the temptations during the fast were intended to get Him to quit the fast.

Jesus was led by the Spirit to fast and pray in that desert before He ever preached one sermon, healed one cripple, freed one captive, or called one disciple. All the while He was sharpening His edge for what was yet to come. At the end of those forty long days and nights in the desert, Satan tested Jesus in three specific areas intended to get Jesus to compromise the path to our redemption. Satan did not want Jesus to succeed at taking back what Adam and Eve had turned over to him when they gave in to their appetites and ate from the tree of the knowledge of good and evil.

If you are born again, Satan knows who you are in Christ. He knows the covenant that was made with the blood of Jesus. He knows that you have authority over all of his power. But he does not have to recognize who you are in Christ as long *you* do not recognize who you are in Christ—all he has to do is tempt you and lead you by your fleshly appetites. We are driven by our flesh far more often than we should be. We want what we want when we want it, and we want it *now*! Fasting "dethrones" the rule of our demanding fleshly appetites so that we can more easily follow the leading of the Holy Spirit.

The wisdom of coming away with the Lord and sharpening our edge indeed brings success. We see it modeled in the life of Jesus more than once. If Jesus needed the power of the Holy Spirit in His life and ministry on Earth, then you and I need that same power all the more. The days are not getting any easier. The church desperately needs to regain the edge for the battles ahead.

> We need the power of the Holy Spirit
> operating in our lives. The Holy Spirit
> knows when we need to fast and pray.

On your sixth day of fasting, remember:

- Spend time waiting on the Lord and listening for His voice today.

- Your senses of smell, touch, and hearing are likely to become heightened.

- You will continue to experience weight loss and detoxification.

Thoughts for your journal:

- How is this fasting experience bringing you closer to God?

- How does the example of Jesus fasting inspire you?

_____

_____

_____

_____

PRAYER FOCUS DAY 6: Preparing for Breakthrough

When Jesus fasted, it helped Him to prepare for the spiritual battles ahead as He stepped out in His earthly ministry. What spiritual battles do you foresee in your life, and how is God preparing you for breakthrough during this fast? What breakthroughs in your personal life, your family, your church, or your community are needed? Pray for a release of God's power to overcome any situation and for supernatural blessings to pour into your life as you prepare to fulfill the destiny He has given you.

Specific breakthrough targets:

_____

_____

_____

_____

_____

> The steps of a good man are ordered by
> the LORD, and He delights in his way.
>
> —PSALM 37:23

A re you living a lifestyle that doesn't allow you to stop and listen to God? Has the unspoken attitude of your heart become one of, "If God has anything to say, He better hurry up and say it"? God is saying to you today:

> You will seek Me and find Me, when you search for Me with all your heart.
>
> —JEREMIAH 29:13

Intimacy cannot be rushed. It must be worked on day by day. Crowds of people often surrounded Jesus, yet He frequently withdrew to get alone with God and pray. He knew that He needed to stay tapped into the Source of all things, and so do we. There is a price to be paid if you want to hear from God and walk in His will.

The problem with most of us is we are too impatient. If God doesn't speak to us in the first five minutes of prayer, we decide He isn't talking today. We have been blighted with a microwave mentality. We want everything now, including maturity. We've deleted from our Bibles the scriptures that command us to wait upon the Lord.

Jesus was waiting on God for forty days and nights as He fasted in the wilderness. God was working on Him. There is a work going on in you right now that you may not be fully aware of, but without fasting, prayer, and wilderness experiences, you will never be qualified to handle what God has for you in the future. Fasting prepares you for what is yet to come!

Fifteen times in the New Testament the Lord says, "He who has an ear, let him hear what the Spirit says." That tells you three important things about hearing. First, you were born into God's family with spiritual ears. Second, having spiritual ears to hear from God is not enough. You also have to learn to use them. Before Jesus ascended into heaven, Luke records that "He opened their understanding, that they might comprehend the Scriptures" (Luke 24:45). They had been hearing the Scriptures all their lives but still did not fully understand them until then. And third, hearing from God must become the highest priority of your life.

Why is it that we can hear from God in crisis better than other times? Because we have to. A crisis moves hearing from God to priority number one. But until hearing from Him is always our first priority, we will keep living from crisis to crisis and never learn to hear from Him correctly. Fasting is slowing down to speed up. It's taking time to listen for your next set of instructions from the throne.

Fasting is not fun. There is not a lot of joy during a fast—but I can assure you there is joy afterward. As we see in Hebrews 4:15–16:

> For we do not have a High Priest who cannot sympathize with our weaknesses, but was in all points tempted as we are, yet without sin. Let us therefore come boldly to the throne of grace, that we may obtain mercy and find grace to help in time of need.

One thing that I believe all Christians must come to realize is if we are going to walk with God, at some point we need to get out of our comfort zone. Life brings extremes. I trust that the Spirit of God has led you into this season of fasting. Continue to follow Him! You will "return in the power of the Spirit" with a fresh rhema word from God for your life. We want everything with a shortcut, but remember there is work to be done. His timing is perfect, and your time will come.

> The power of the Holy Spirit is the edge
> we need to endure. Jesus sent the Holy
> Spirit to dwell with us and to dwell in
> us to lead and empower us to do the
> greater works He prepared for us to do.

On your seventh day of fasting, remember:

- Make sure you're drinking enough water.

- Take time to rest and relax as you wait upon the Lord today.

- Continue to meditate and listen for that still, small voice.

Thoughts for your journal:

- Have you ever had a sense of God speaking to you, and if so, how did you know it was God's voice?

- What are the different ways you expect God to speak to you during this fast?

_____

_____

_____

PRAYER FOCUS DAY 7: Be Still and Know

In your prayer time today, focus more on listening than on talking to God. Sit and wait quietly for Him to speak. Whether this is a new practice for you or not, you're likely to be surprised as you sense His presence and leading. The Bible says, "Be still, and know that I am God" (Ps. 46:10). As you find time to be still in His presence today, realize that He *is* God and He has everything in your life under control. He does have a purpose for you, and He wants you to be fully prepared for it. He knows what you need and how to provide it for you. Trust in Him as you wait upon Him today.

Record what you sense God is saying to you as you seek Him:

_____

_____

_____

_____

> He who comes to God must believe
> that He is, and that He is a rewarder of
> those who diligently seek Him.
>
> —HEBREWS 11:6

Brokenness is so precious in the eyes of the Lord. God responds to brokenness, but not so He can rush in and save the day like some kind of cartoon hero. Brokenness makes room for Him to release His strength through our weakness in order to accomplish His plans. That is a crucial difference that we need to understand.

> The LORD is near to those who have a broken heart,
> And saves such as have a contrite spirit.
>
> —PSALM 34:18

Remember the story of God speaking to Moses from the burning bush? It's found in chapters 3 and 4 of the Book of Exodus. God disrupted Moses's daily routine with a sight he had never seen before, a big bush that was on fire but was not consumed by the flames. When Moses made a point to stop what he was doing, turn, and investigate, God began to speak with him.

Forty years earlier Moses fled Egypt a broken and confused man. His pride and zeal had led him to murder an Egyptian who was beating a fellow Hebrew. By the next day Moses's own people had turned on him, as did the king of Egypt, who desired to kill him. He escaped into the desert where he later married, started a family, and began herding sheep. He buried himself in his new identity and profession, right down to the shepherd's rod that he carried at all times. That rod was not only a tool, but it also symbolized what he did and who he was—his security. Even so, it was just a dead stick. God had the needs of a bigger flock in mind when He stopped Moses that day, the day Moses's brokenness was complete.

The cries of the Hebrew people had come to the attention of the Lord. It was time to commission and equip Moses to carry out His plan to deliver the people of Israel from the oppressive bondage of slavery in Egypt. Moses couldn't fathom how in the world his Hebrew brethren would ever believe him. He questioned how God could possibly use him with all his limitations and his horrible past. So God instructed Moses to throw down the rod he held in his hand. When he dropped that stick, releasing that symbol of his identity and his own strength, God gave him a startling demonstration of His ability to work with even a dead stick in order to serve His purposes! Moses, a broken man, was filled with the power and presence of the Lord, and the people in bondage were set free.

It is not a coincidence that the meekest man in the Bible was one who fasted. Moses fasted for forty days, and God used him to lead His people to freedom.

> Most of us struggle with the concept
> that it is our own strength that draws
> God's attention, when our strength is
> the very last thing God notices.

On your eighth day of fasting, remember:

- Continue to spend time quietly listening to God.

- As you continue to forsake the flesh for a chance to hear God's voice, you'll enter what I call the "sweet spot"—a place that feels as though you've walked right into the holy of holies.

Thoughts for your journal:

- Do you tend to try to accomplish God's plans in your own strength?

- How does acknowledging your weakness help you truly accomplish His plans?

_____

_____

_____

PRAYER FOCUS DAY 8: Welcome Brokenness

What are God's purposes in the earth today? Are people in bondage today, desperate for freedom and an end to the torture and suffering, crying out to a God they don't even know? Does He desire to use us to break their chains? Yes and yes! The real question is this: Will you and I interrupt our lives and our routines—even our religious routines—enough to regain the edge and truly become broken before the Lord so that He can use us to reach them? The brokenness that comes through fasting starts with throwing everything we identify as our strength down at the feet of Jesus to say, "Lord, I know I am limited. I'm coming to You in brokenness, not in my strength but in my weakness. I acknowledge that You can do more through me, broken, than I can ever attempt to do on my own." That is the type of fasting that connects with God.

List the things you need God's strength to accomplish:

_____

_____

_____

_____

> And He said to me, "My grace is sufficient for you,
> for My strength is made perfect in weakness."
>
> —2 CORINTHIANS 12:9

Fasting is not just another religious exercise. This journal opens with a passage about fasting from Isaiah 58, but if you read Isaiah 58 carefully, you see that the chapter actually begins with God rebuking the people who were fasting because their form of fasting was merely a mundane outward display to demonstrate their religiosity. Of their hypocrisy God said:

> Is such a fast as yours what I have chosen, a day for a man to humble himself with sorrow in his soul? [Is true fasting merely mechanical?] Is it only to bow down his head like a bulrush and to spread sackcloth and ashes under him [to indicate a condition of heart that he does not have]? Will you call this a fast and an acceptable day to the Lord?
>
> —Isaiah 58:5, amp

God saw right through that religious fast as just another routine! Fasting is supposed to break the routine, not become another passionless performance. The Amplified Bible uses the term "bulrush" in this passage, referring to a tall, grassy reed that grew along rivers. It was hollow on the inside, so it would easily bow down with its own weight, similar in appearance to someone bowing down in hollow humility. It reminds me of the mechanical bulls that became popular in the 1980s. They were originally designed for rodeo riders to use for practice, but they quickly caught on as a form of entertainment for "wannabe" cowboys and cowgirls everywhere. Even though those things can be engineered to imitate nearly all the moves of a real bucking bull—they are only mechanical. They go through the motions, but they're not the real deal.

God is looking for the real deal! If we are not careful, every one of us can grow hardened to the Spirit of God and indifferent in our worship, mechanically going through the motions with no brokenness, no passion. It is easy for Christians to cruise along through life in a dull routine. Perhaps you added another zero to your salary this year…but there was a time when you didn't have anything and tears would flow as you worshiped. The more He does for us, the more thankful we should be—not the more relaxed and comfortable. If you are cruising along in a dull, passionless routine, it is time to break the routine. That's what fasting—true fasting—does. Fasting clears the way for us to refocus and hear the heart of God. As I've said before, fasting is a short-term discipline that yields long-term effects. Fasting is a choice you and I can make to interrupt "life as usual" in order to hear what God wants to do and how He wants to use us to make a difference in someone else's life.

Men, women, and children desperately cry out for help every day, all over the world, in this country, perhaps even right down the street. They are in bondage. They are abused, oppressed, misused, hungry, alone, forgotten, and crushed. We may not be able to hear their cries—but you can believe that God does. He hears the cry of the oppressed and the unsaved. That is why the fast God desires is not an empty, passionless religious act that bears no fruit. God cannot bless that. God has a specific purpose for fasting and prayer.

> I've learned that it is dangerous to have a growing ministry and at the same time have shrinking passion for God. It is dangerous for whatever your focus is to get bigger on the outside, while inside your passion for God has grown cold.

On your ninth day of fasting, remember:

- Spend extended time reading God's Word today.

- Try a short walk outdoors or do some other light activity if you need a breath of fresh air.

Thoughts for your journal:

- Reflect on the past twelve months of your life, or the time since your last fast.

- In what ways have you been settling for mediocrity in your Christian walk?

PRAYER FOCUS DAY 9: Get Real

It's time to get serious about sharpening your edge—and fasting is the way to do it. You are a spiritual gatekeeper in your own life and in your home. If you've been lulled into a life of going through the motions, chances are you've let down your guard and allowed some things into your life that shouldn't be there. What have you been harboring on the inside that you wouldn't want to be exposed on the outside? Spend your prayer time today asking God to show you what you need to change as you put an end to ho-hum Christianity and start living an authentic life of faith that draws others to Christ.

What things do you need to change as you regain your edge?

_____

_____

_____

_____

> The LORD does not see as man sees; for
> man looks at the outward appearance,
> but the LORD looks at the heart.
>
> —1 SAMUEL 16:7

Think about what took place when Jesus and the disciples traveled through Samaria on their way to Galilee. They stopped at the well in the Samarian town of Sychar. The disciples were hungry, so they went into the city to buy some food, but Jesus decided to stay at the well. When a local woman walked up to get some water, Jesus asked her for water. Since Jews didn't speak to Samaritans, that was the first thing that surprised the woman about Him.

But it wasn't the last. Jesus began to tell her things about her life, like how many times she had been married and the fact that the man she currently lived with was not her husband. The Lord's insights into her life prompted her to acknowledge that He must be a prophet, so she responded as so many of us tend to do: she started religious discussion in the hopes of deflecting His attention off of her. She hoped that turning the discussion to the long-standing debate between Samaritans and Jews over whether one must worship in Jerusalem or on the mountain in Samaria where her people had worshiped since the time of Jacob would do the trick. But again Jesus brought the attention back to her and the fact that she was not worshiping at either location with her whole heart. He told her:

> The hour is coming, and now is, when the true worshipers will worship the Father in spirit and truth; for the Father is seeking such to worship Him. God is Spirit, and those who worship Him must worship in spirit and truth.
>
> —JOHN 4:23–24

The disciples came back about that time, and though they wondered why Jesus was going against custom to talk to a woman, they chose not to ask. When Jesus told the woman that He was the Messiah, she got too excited to care about getting water from the well. She left her jar behind as she ran into town telling everyone what she'd just experienced. Samaritans only followed the first five books of the Bible. They didn't yet have the whole truth.

But they were hungry. They desired more. When the men of her town heard her words, they went out to see Jesus for themselves. Notice that when the disciples went to town, they didn't bring back someone who needed to be healed. They didn't bring back someone they had raised from the dead or a demoniac they had set free. The only thing they brought back was lunch. When the Samaritan woman went to town, the whole town followed her back! The disciples brought Jesus a Happy Meal, but she brought Him souls!

Some of our churches have become like that today— we have no room for more. We sit and receive until we are full to our ears, belching in our "La-Z-Boy" pews with our "remote controls" flipping through what we do and don't like in a service, so stuffed that we have no room for more and no passion for Jesus. If the twelve apostles could miss it, you and I are certainly capable of taking for granted the goodness of the Lord. We can easily become so full of ourselves that we must be emptied through fasting and prayer, seeking the Lord in brokenness. I believe with all of my heart that God is looking for people who will not lose their passion—people He can bless in abundance, and the more He blesses them, the hungrier, the more passionate they will become and the more kingdom power will be released as a result.

It is amazing to me that everything Jesus endured through His trial, through His beating, through His crucifixion—is called His *passion*. Power follows passion! That applies to so many areas. If you are standing in a worship service and it doesn't seem to have any power, remember that power follows passion. Is there any passion in the worship, or is it just routine? Is there any passion in the preaching, or is it another dull sermon? When one person can break through with passion, power can be released.

Where there is hunger, there is passion. Where there is passion, there is power.

> Whenever we see the release of power
> in the Bible, it follows someone not
> caring what others thought.

On your tenth day of fasting, remember:

- Let your physical hunger pangs remind you to pray for a deeper spiritual hunger today.

- Drink plenty of water.

Thoughts for your journal:

- What things have you allowed to fill your heart?

- What steps can you take to make room for the things of God that have been crowded out?

PRAYER FOCUS DAY 10: God's Power in You

Spiritual hunger is the first step to a powerful life. Hunger leads to passion, and passion leads to power. How long has it been since you've hungered for the things of God? As you experience physical hunger today, ask God to give you a new spiritual hunger. Dive into His Word and ask for His power to be demonstrated in your life. If you've become "full" of the comforts or cares of this life, make room in your heart for the things of God today. Empty yourself of everything that is not of God. Hunger for more and more of His presence and power as you regain your edge through fasting today.

Express your newly revived passion for God:

_____

_____

_____

_____

> As the deer pants for the water brooks,
> so pants my soul for You, O God.
>
> —PSALM 42:1

D o you feel like you have wasted far too much of your life for God to do anything through you? Maybe you think that of a loved one whom you have tried for years to reach and the enemy wants you to think it's a big waste of time. I want to make it perfectly clear that you are perfectly wrong in that thinking. In God's hands nothing is wasted. The Bible says the prodigal son "gathered up all that he had and journeyed into a distant country, and there he wasted his fortune in reckless and loose [from restraint] living" (Luke 15:13, AMP). But the day came when there was the return of the waster. He came to his senses, and his father restored him completely.

Have you spent your life wasted on drugs, on alcohol? Have you wasted your years by abusing your body with sexual addictions? Fasting can break the yoke of the waster. It takes courage to say, "I have an addiction in my life, and I need to be free." But Jesus knows that you have wasted enough of your life, and it is time to be made completely new. If you are struggling with an addiction, fast and pray…seek the Lord in your brokenness. Nothing is hidden from His sight. He knows everything about you. He can cleanse you. He can fill you with His love. He will remove that burden and repair what has been wasted.

Maybe you know someone who is hooked on drugs, alcohol, or some other kind of vice. I urge you to use today's fast to cry out to God on their behalf. Gather up the fragments of that person's wasted life as you fast and pray for his or her deliverance. God wants nothing wasted! Is your life cluttered with fragments and broken pieces? Take them to the Lord. Lay them at His feet. Let Him restore and rebuild and fill you with His passion. God cares about the fragments and pieces of your life!

If you are a parent, has the enemy convinced you that you have never had a good relationship with your kids, you never will, and it's a waste of time to try? Or maybe he's whispered that you will never mend the relationship with your parents, your spouse, or your siblings because too much stuff has been said and been done. You have become convinced that the hurt runs so deep that they will never speak to you again. I believe when you fast according to what God calls a fast, you will "not hide yourself from your own flesh" (Isa. 58:7). In other words, the walls that have divided you will crumble as every wall of resistance begins to weaken. While you fast and pray, ask God to restore what the enemy has taken from your family. Pray that lines of communication that have been destroyed between your own flesh-and-blood relatives will be restored. God says:

> Those from among you shall build the old waste places; you shall raise up the foundations of many generations; and you shall be called the Repairer of the Breach; the Restorer of Streets to Dwell In.
>
> —ISAIAH 58:12

Once you are free, God can use you like a well-lit street to lead others to Him. He can use you like a bridge to reach those who are distant from Him. Through you He can take those lives that have been desolate and destroyed by addictions, oppression, and abuse and turn what was once a wasteland into a fruitful garden.

> When it comes to fasting and praying for your marriage and family relationships, don't give up. There may be nothing you can do...but there is nothing He cannot do.

On your eleventh day of fasting, remember:

- Go to your prayer time and prayer place.

- Make sure you get enough rest and water.

- The Lord's presence continues to become more apparent the longer you continue your fast.

Thoughts for your journal:

- What are some things you feel the enemy has stolen from you? Your dreams? Health? Relationships? Financial security? Begin to ask the Lord to restore these things to you.

- How do you think God, in His eternal perspective, sees the times or areas in your life that you're tempted to think of as wasted?

PRAYER FOCUS DAY 11: Restoration

Today is the day to declare: "No more wasted time. No more stolen years, relationships, health, or resources in my life." As you pray today, give it all to God. The Lord responds to your brokenness when you tell Him, "Lord, I give You my heart and soul; You are the only one I live for. With every breath I take, Lord, I want You to have Your way in me." And then let Him show Himself strong through your life. He can restore everything the enemy has stolen from your life and your family. He is a master at picking up broken pieces and making something beautiful out of them. Ask God to give you a new perspective on the things you feel have been wasted or stolen.

What is God showing you about restoration in your life?

_____

_____

_____

> Return to the stronghold, you prisoners of hope. Even today I declare that I will restore double to you.
>
> —ZECHARIAH 9:12

Sometimes you can pray for something, but you don't see the answer right away. Keep praying. Don't let go of your faith, and do not cast aside your confidence! It may be that the thing you are praying for is just not ready or in God's timing yet. Your prayers will not be ignored or discarded. Prayers don't have an expiration date!

The Book of Revelation even refers to bowls of incense collected in heaven that are the prayers of the saints. Daniel had been fasting and praying for three weeks when the angel of the Lord appeared to him, explaining how his prayers had been heard in heaven since the first day, but the answer had been delayed:

> Then he said to me, "Do not fear, Daniel, for from the first day that you set your heart to understand, and to humble yourself before your God, your words were heard; and I have come because of your words. But the prince of the kingdom of Persia withstood me twenty-one days; and behold, Michael, one of the chief princes, came to help me, for I had been left alone there with the kings of Persia. Now I have come to make you understand what will happen to your people in the latter days, for the vision refers to many days yet to come."
>
> —DANIEL 10:12–14

Acts chapter 10 is one of the most powerful chapters in the Bible. Prior to the events detailed in that chapter, only the Jews had received the good news of the gospel and the baptism of the Holy Spirit. But everything changed when one man's hunger and persistence penetrated heaven. Peter went up on the roof of his friend Simon's house to pray. He was hungry because it was lunchtime. But once again, when man was thinking about sinking his teeth into a big, juicy, well-done kosher steak, God had a far different plan for lunch!

One day earlier, an angel visited a devout Italian man who loved God. The man's prayers and giving had come up as a memorial before God. He was a Gentile, but he and his household believed in God and wanted to know Him. At the end of four days of prayer, and perhaps even fasting, the angel of the Lord appeared to this man named Cornelius and told him to send for a man named Peter. Cornelius's men headed out and arrived the next day while Peter was on the roof—receiving a vision about food of all things! God was using food to show Peter that He desired to pour out His Spirit on *all* flesh, including the Gentiles. The Gentiles included every one who was not of Jewish descent and were long considered by Jewish law to be unclean.

Two men, miles apart, became connected by hunger. Cornelius was praying with a hunger for God. Peter was on a roof at lunchtime receiving a message from God about food instead of chowing down on lunch.

One man was seeking; one man had the answer. Both men were praying, and a connection was made. Before they ever met physically, their prayers met in heaven. I think that is so powerful! Cornelius was storing up prayer in heaven. The next day (no expiration date on prayer) the Spirit of the Lord prepared Peter for his role in what had already been decreed in heaven. When Peter went up on that roof to pray at lunchtime, God made the prayer connection, opening the door of salvation to the Gentiles.

I want you to understand that heaven has kingdom connections for you. When you pray, your prayers plug into God's connection of plans, resources, and power in heaven. All over this world there are connections that God is setting up—things we have no idea about, but by simply following the prompting of the Holy Spirit's call to fast, we take part in divinely orchestrated connections.

Notice that Cornelius's prayers "sizzled" in heaven for a while before the connection came to pass. In fact, the angel even told him that his prayers and generosity had come up as a memorial before God.

Do you have loved ones who need divine connections? Do you need godly connections in your own life? Sharpen your edge and start stacking up prayers.

> When you pray in alignment with God's will, He hears. You can rest assured that you have set something in motion in the supernatural even if you are not able to discern them in the natural.

On your twelfth day of fasting, remember:

- Hunger is still an issue, but stay focused on God.

- Continue to journal your journey.

Thoughts for your journal:

- Think of a time when you felt as if God wasn't answering your prayers. Looking back, can you see how He intervened in that situation for your good, even though you couldn't see it at the time? Write about this situation, and reflect on it to increase your faith for your current prayer needs.

Making Prayer Connections

All over the world today God hears the cries of the unsaved, the cries of the abused, the oppressed, the captive, those who follow false gods. But here's the deal: there needs to be a prayer connection! As you give up your meals today, you can be that prayer connection. As you continue to heed the Spirit's leading to fast from food and entertainment today in order to dine instead on doing the will of God, pray that His work will be finished in someone else's life. I pray that God will link your physical hunger to the spiritual hunger of drug addicts, alcoholics, the brokenhearted, the down-and-out as well as the up-and-in millionaire who has everything but Jesus.

List the people for whom you are stacking up prayers:

_____

_____

_____

> Confess your trespasses to one another, and pray for
> one another, that you may be healed. The effective,
> fervent prayer of a righteous man avails much.
>
> —JAMES 5:16

Yesterday I talked about stacking up prayer connections in your family's lives and your life. There is another way that fasting and praying make an important prayer connection in your life—to God's assignment. I know this personally because I was on a fast when the Lord made my assignment clear, calling me to preach. Up to that point I was seriously considering a career in music. In the nearly twenty-five years since that time, He has continued to give me specific "alignment for assignments" during a fast. Many developments in my life and ministry since then have been made clear as I have continued to fast and pray, seeking God's direction.

I mentioned yesterday that Peter and Cornelius made a prayer connection, and both discovered God's assignment. Peter was to break the long-held divide between Jew and Gentile by sharing what God had given him with Cornelius and his family. But it didn't end there. Another connection was coming that would give us nearly half of the books of the New Testament.

A young man named Saul watched as Stephen, a follower of Jesus who was full of the Holy Spirit, was dragged from the synagogue and brutally stoned to death outside of the city. As a young Hebrew devoted to the Law, this incident fueled Saul's desire to stamp out the dangerous "sect" that followed Jesus even after His death. Acts 8:3 reads, "As for Saul, he made havoc of the church, entering every house, and dragging off men and women, committing them to prison." On his way to the city of Damascus with permission from the high priest to arrest any followers he encountered, Saul's world was turned upside down. He found way more than he planned to on that trip when he met *the* High Priest! As the story continues in Acts 9, Saul was knocked to the ground and engulfed by a bright light. He heard the voice of a man speaking. When he humbly asked who was speaking to him, he heard, "I am Jesus, whom you are persecuting" (v. 5).

At that moment Saul lost his sight and had to be led by his men the rest of the way to Damascus. He fasted there for three days, no doubt praying and pondering the unmistakable encounter he'd had on the road. But the Lord didn't leave him like that. He had a connection planned. Fasting got him in alignment for his assignment.

Across town there lived a man named Ananias who was hungry for God and eager to serve. In a vision he received instructions to find Saul, who had already been told that Ananias would be coming. Ananias was instructed to lay hands on Saul's eyes so that he could receive his sight again. After that connection was made, Saul went immediately from persecuting Christians to becoming one, and went on to preach the truth of God's Word to the Jews and especially to the Gentiles. After changing his name to Paul, he went from being full of religious zeal to being full of passion for Jesus. He wrote to his Hebrew brethren in Rome:

> My heart's desire and prayer to God for Israel is that they may be saved. For I bear them witness that they have a zeal for God, but not according to knowledge. For they being ignorant of God's righteousness, and seeking to establish their own righteousness, have not submitted to the righteousness of God. For Christ is the end of the law for righteousness to everyone who believes.
> —ROMANS 10:1–4

> **Fasting puts you in alignment for your assignment.**

On your thirteenth day of fasting, remember:

- Keep drinking enough water.

- Continue to pray and meditate on God's Word.

- Be ready for cravings to return.

Thoughts for your journal:

- If this is the first time you've ever fasted, are you sensing a clearer direction from God than you ever have before? Explain.

- If you aren't new to fasting, can you remember other times of fasting that preceded major God assignments in your life? Describe them.

_____

_____

_____

PRAYER FOCUS DAY 13: Alignment for Your Assignment

Could there be other "Pauls" out there just waiting for God's connection to be made? Could you be the one God will use to drop the scales from their eyes? When you fast and pray, you connect with God's assignment for your life, those "good works" that God has prepared for us to walk in. When you don't fast and pray, you do not connect with God's assignment. I love the fact that we get our assignment from God when we break out of the routine and seek Him in prayer and fasting. We can connect so God can direct our lives. It is time to quit worrying about everything and pray. When you pray, your prayer becomes the "plug" that plugs into God's resources.

Record any assignments you sense God is giving you:

_____

_____

_____

_____

> Trust in the LORD with all your heart, and lean
> not on your own understanding; in all your ways
> acknowledge Him, and He shall direct your paths.
>
> —PROVERBS 3:5–6

One of the things the enemy hates most about fasting is persistence. That is why I love longer fasts like our annual twenty-one-day fast. When you make it through the first few days of his lies telling you that you can't make it—you get stronger and the resistance becomes weaker. When Jesus ended His forty-day fast, the Bible says the devil fled from Him. It has now been two weeks that you have persisted in this fast. You are entering the final stretch, and nothing can hold you back.

I believe that is how some of the miracles we read about in God's Word came about—through persistence. Think about the story of the woman who had been bleeding for years in Luke chapter 8. Doctors could do nothing to help her. She was considered "unclean" by the people of her time and basically ignored unless she came near a crowd, who would then move away from her for fear of contamination. But she heard about Jesus. Even though she was outcast, even if she had to crawl, she would not be denied the opportunity to touch at least the very edge of His garment. Who would know? And maybe, just maybe, her healing would come forth. So she pressed, she persisted, she made her way through the mob that surrounded Jesus that day, and with a shaking arm, she reached her dirty fingers out to grasp the edge of His robe.

She quickly let go, no doubt overwhelmed by the warmth of God's love that began to flow through her body and heal what was wrong with her. She felt the power of the Lord because of her persistence—and He felt her! He felt power leave Him and stopped everything to find out who it was. Luke wrote:

> Now when the woman saw that she was not hidden, she came trembling; and falling down before Him, she declared to Him in the presence of all the people the reason she had touched Him and how she was healed immediately.
>
> —Luke 8:47

When you pray and fast, your persistence breaks resistance. It brings you to a place where you can feel God move powerfully in your life—but it also causes Him to feel your need, just as He felt the woman who needed healing touch Him in the midst of that huge crowd. Whatever forces have been resisting what God had coming in your life, your persistence will break resistance.

Regardless of whether you gave your life to Jesus eighty years ago or if you just got saved eight minutes ago, it is not too late to start stacking up prayers in heaven! If your family is in shambles, I assure you that it is not too late for you to fast and pray to ask God to intervene! It is time to be persistent and break down the resistance.

> Fasting not only positions you to feel God—but it also positions you for Him to hear your heart's cry as well.

On your fourteenth day of fasting, remember:

- Play your favorite worship music.

- Continue listening for God's voice as you wait upon Him.

- Weight loss continues.

Thoughts for your journal:

- Look up scriptures that address how God's Word says He will meet the specific needs in your life. Begin to pray those

scriptures in faith and apply them to your situation. Write
them here.

_____

_____

_____

_____

PRAYER FOCUS DAY 14: Health and Healing

You may have heard of the PUSH prayer model: Pray Until Something
Happens. It's a good reminder to be persistent in prayer. You may
have other areas that need persistent prayer in your life, but today, if there
is sickness in your body or mind, or in the body or mind of a loved one,
begin to speak forth health and healing in Jesus's name. Begin to declare
that you are healed, and don't give up. You may have been praying for
this healing for years. Keep praying! You may feel discouraged, especially
if you are living with pain. But Jehovah-Rapha, the healing One, is your
God. Begin to declare what His Word says about healing. Your persistence
will break the resistance, just like the woman with the issue of blood. Her
healing came about because she persisted and positioned herself where she
could touch the Master. By your prayers today, position yourself to touch
the Master. Speak words that release health and healing for your body, your
family, your church, and others.

Prayer requests:

> Continue earnestly in prayer, being
> vigilant in it with thanksgiving.
>
> —COLOSSIANS 4:2

It can be so easy to come up with reasons not to fast or to cut short a fast after you have started—especially when it comes to jobs, sports, our overly worshiped entertainment, and, last but not least, convenience. Fasting breaks the routine, and that is *in*convenient. But like that old John Wayne movie, it takes "true grit" to submit yourself to God through fasting and prayer and to turn from the things of this world. Take a closer look at what James had to say about "humbling ourselves":

> Whoever therefore wants to be a friend of the world makes himself an enemy of God. Or do you think that the Scripture says in vain, "The Spirit who dwells in us yearns jealously"? But He gives more grace. Therefore He says: "God resists the proud, but gives grace to the humble." Therefore submit to God. Resist the devil and he will flee from you. Draw near to God and He will draw near to you. Cleanse your hands, you sinners; and purify your hearts, you double-minded. Lament and mourn and weep! Let your laughter be turned to mourning and your joy to gloom. Humble yourselves in the sight of the Lord, and He will lift you up.
>
> —James 4:4–10

That sounds very much like an invitation to fast! James makes it pretty clear that we can either submit to God or submit to the world. Likewise, we are either resisting the devil or resisting God. If we are not drawing closer to God, we are drifting farther from Him. Fasting is a choice to break the allure of the world and all its trappings as we put our flesh under submission. When you turn from the things of the world and submit yourself to God, He will give you the grace to stand strong and resist the temptations of the enemy. Especially on an extended fast like this twenty-one-day fast, you will discover that time spent fasting, praying, and meditating on God's

Word cleanses and purifies your heart and focuses your thoughts on things above rather than the stuff of this world.

God calls us to be sober-minded, to get focused on His purposes, and to trust His grace. Fasting is not happy hour. Fasting is a time when you embrace emptiness. You become more and more sensitive to the Spirit of God, often to the point where weeping is the only expression of what is happening inside your heart.

It takes work to get your flesh under submission. Paul explained that the flesh wars against the Spirit—and the Spirit wars against the flesh. So you need to ask yourself: Which one are you empowering? Which one are you giving access to control your life?

I understand that sometimes on a fast you can't hear God speak over the sound of your stomach growling. I've been there! You can't focus on your morning devotions for thinking about oatmeal. (It is amazing how, during an extended fast, even the most bland foods sound wonderful. Food you would normally pass over on a breakfast buffet suddenly sounds like fine dining.) You want to read the Word, but you have a headache; you are cold and probably tired from the toxins being filtered out of your body. You might feel like you are just physically falling apart, but stay the course and don't let your flesh or the devil shortchange your reward!

Now you can see why Paul so urgently warns us to "walk in the Spirit, and you shall not fulfill the lust of the flesh" (Gal. 5:16). You *can* be victorious in the battle between your flesh and spirit—and fasting, prayer, and feeding your spirit on God's Word will help accelerate the process.

When you wait on the Lord, He will give you strong wings to soar beyond your limitations. As you wait, you will strengthen your inner man, becoming more and more aware of your authority in Christ Jesus over the devil.

On your fifteenth day of fasting, remember:

- Stay hydrated.

- Spend extra time in praise and worship today.

- Don't allow hunger to cause you to lose focus on God.

Thoughts for your journal:

- When you fast, quiet yourself. Get still by turning off the crazy distractions of this life and press into God's presence. Open God's Word and devour it. God will speak to you through His Word. The Bible contains the answer to every dilemma you face, and if you will read it as you fast, God will speak to you.

PRAYER FOCUS DAY 15: Don't Give In to Your Flesh!

Encourage yourself in prayer today that your time in fasting is not wasted. You are regaining your edge, and you will take the enemy out! Read the scripture from Isaiah 40 below. As you wait on the Lord today, envision Him renewing your strength and giving you wings. Whether you need those wings to regain your hope from a tragic situation, or you need them for your dreams to take flight, you must wait on Him and sharpen your edge. There may be situations in your life, your ministry, your calling, your business, or your marriage where it seems like Satan is so deeply entrenched he will never be ousted. Don't believe the lie. Fast, pray, and wait upon the Lord. As you do, you will change your inner man to line up with God's will. Think about that when the enemy tempts you to give up on this fast, and determine that this is the time to press in like never before.

What will you do while you wait on the Lord today?

_____

_____

> But those who wait on the LORD shall renew their strength; they shall mount up with wings like eagles, they shall run and not be weary, they shall walk and not faint.
>
> —ISAIAH 40:31

When you draw closer to God, He draws closer to you. In the same way, when you get serious with God, He gets serious with you.

When you choose to fast, fast with a cause. Deep in your heart, determine the reason you're fasting, and then write down your cause. It is important to keep your focus. What is on your heart for this fast? Is it for your family? Is it your desire to draw closer to God? Is it the need for financial breakthrough? Is it for a healing? Are you fasting because you are afraid and have so many problems surrounding you that you don't know what else to do?

Define your reason, and then write it down. I'm sure you didn't enter this fast casually, with a hit-or-miss attitude, or you would have failed by now. Every time you fast, pray and ask God what He wants you to do. Prayerfully determine the length and type of fast, and then write down the day you will begin and the day you will end. Ask for His grace and mercy to endure as you begin.

There are two powers at work when you fast: the human will and the supernatural power of God. When you decide to exercise your will and put your flesh under submission to the Spirit of God, His supernatural power kicks in and helps you fast according to the level of the commitment that you have made. You can do far more in the anointing of God than you can in human zeal. God's anointing is not for thrills—it is for battle. When you go into battle, you fight to win. The anointing that comes through fasting and prayer gives you a fresh strength to fight for your family, for your kids, for your marriage, and to win! It gives you the ability to hear God's heart and pray forth those things that He desires to release in the nations.

You cannot do God's will with human zeal any more than you can effectively chop down a huge oak tree with a dull ax. Most of the time you will cause more damage than good by not waiting upon the Lord for His way,

His direction, and His anointing. Take the time to sit down and work on sharpening that edge. That is what fasting does. It helps you get your edge back. It is a process that takes time.

Yesterday you started the third week of this twenty-one-day fast—but you're not done. If we compare the three weeks of your fast to the three steps involved in sharpening an ax, we've already passed through the first week, what I often call "the grind"—the first step of sharpening an ax that files down the bigger, uneven sections of the ax head. In the second week, or middle step of ax sharpening, we've used a smooth stone to polish and hone the steel to a razor-fine edge. This final week is the third step in getting your edge back. In our ax-sharpening metaphor, this step is when we take the oil and gently rub it from the top to the bottom of that sharp blade in order to get all the fragments, shavings, and dirt off of it. You could think about that "DIRT" as an acronym:

- D—Disobedience

- I—Ignorance (zeal without knowledge)

- R—Rebellion

- T—The tongue (words of doubt and unbelief)

Then you are ready to swing that ax under the anointing of the Lord!

> If you're casual about your fast, God
> will be casual about it too.

On your sixteenth day of fasting, remember:

- Combat mood swings by focusing on how this fast is helping you grow spiritually.

- Fasting is a form of worship that will humble you. Remind yourself of your dependency on God.

Thoughts for your journal:

- Reflect on situations in God's Word that seemed impossible without the anointing of God's Spirit.

- What is on your heart as you walk through the final week of this fast? Are there new things you've become aware of and new priorities God has shifted into your focus? Write them down.

_____

_____

_____

_____

_____

PRAYER FOCUS DAY 16: Out With Zeal, in With Anointing

Our zeal can become a stumbling block based in our own pride. God needs empty vessels—not ones so full of themselves that He can't pour Himself out through them. As you pray today, ask God for help if you've been trying to accomplish His will with self-sufficient, arrogant zeal. Human zeal puts on a good show but accomplishes nothing in the Spirit. Give up your striving, let your weakness bring you to your knees, and allow His Spirit to fill you and replenish your spirit and your authority in Christ. Pray until you feel that authority. Pray until the Spirit touches you and fills you afresh.

Remind yourself of the reasons you entered into this fast:

_____

_____

_____

> It is not good to have zeal without knowledge,
> nor to be hasty and miss the way.
>
> —PROVERBS 19:2, NIV

It doesn't take long for anyone to lose his or her edge looking at the condition of the US economy these days. Most of us "over-forty-somethings" can remember the Nixon/Ford/Carter presidency days of the seventies. Nixon's decisions kicked off a rough decade, starting with a devalued dollar and lower gold prices, followed by peak unemployment and recession, ending with peak inflation and angry gas lines. I remember those gas lines. Even as a kid I could sense the insecurity that my family felt regarding the economy in those days. Kids today have watched as their mom and dad have lost their jobs—and many have lost their homes to foreclosure—all at record rates. People have seen their savings run out and their investments plunge almost overnight in some cases. My heart has been heavy as I've witnessed the economy in America sink deeper into crisis. But I want to encourage you—now more than ever—to believe God for His provision. I see evidence throughout Scripture that the men and women of God who pressed in with fasting and prayer, even in difficult times, flourished. God provides. He provides because He is faithful to His Word. He promised:

> The righteous shall flourish like a palm tree
> He shall grow like a cedar in Lebanon.
> Those who are planted in the house of the LORD
> Shall flourish in the courts of our God.
> They shall still bear fruit in old age;
> They shall be fresh and flourishing,
> To declare that the LORD is upright;
> He is my rock, and there is no unrighteousness in Him.
> —PSALM 92:12–15

I don't know about you, but I take much more comfort and place much more faith in the promises of God than I do in the promises of government—any government! Most species of palm trees grow in desert climates. They become firmly rooted even in shifting sand, by design. They tolerate high temperatures, little rainfall, and high winds. And I really like this part: palm trees produce better fruit in their old age. Palms can flourish where other trees would wither and die, and God promises that the righteous, those in right standing with Him, will flourish where others would wither. God designed the root system of palms differently than that of most other trees. Instead of the roots tapering and becoming smaller the farther away they get from the trunk, they stay about the same size. So these big, thick roots make their way far below the hot, dry shifting sands and lock into the nutrient-providing solid foundation below. Not only that, but unlike most trees that have a woody-dead outer layer, the entire trunk of a palm is alive, allowing it to be very flexible, bending with even hurricane-force winds.

Storms will come. Some storms are transitional in nature. Transition is a season that few enjoy because of the storms it unleashes. I believe fasting is necessary to help us sink our roots ever deeper into the solid foundation of God's promises so that we can withstand the storms as they come and continue to be fruitful.

> People who flourish in troubled times
> have been used to change destinies.

On your seventeenth day of fasting, remember:

- Meditate on what this fast means to you.

- Continue to drink enough water.

- Document your thoughts in your journal.

Thoughts for your journal:

- It's impossible this side of heaven to know the full impact of our prayers on the destinies of others and vice versa. What are some of the glimpses of this impact that you may have already seen?

_____

_____

_____

_____

_____

PRAYER FOCUS DAY 17: Not Only Survive, but Thrive

Spending time in fasting and prayer—regardless of your circum-stances—is what will help you be rooted and grounded in your faith, ready to weather any storm of the economy, your health, your family, or your job. Pray for God to use you to flourish even during tough times so that you can change destinies. God has promised that He will cause the righteous to flourish, to build, to expand their territory even in troublesome times! Even when the economy is crashing, as you fast, pray, and seek God's face, you will receive wisdom, plans, and resources to endure and overcome.

Is God giving you a plan to flourish during hard times? Write it down.

_____

_____

_____

_____

> As you have therefore received Christ Jesus the
> Lord, so walk in Him, rooted and built up in Him
> and established in the faith, as you have been
> taught, abounding in it with thanksgiving.
>
> —COLOSSIANS 2:6–7

W e cannot focus on fasting and prayer and expect to get far when we have the wrong understanding of Jesus. We need to cultivate a genuine hunger and thirst for the Lord!

When you hunger and thirst after Jesus, you will be filled. Ultimately, life just does not work unless you believe that He is the Son of God, the Bread of Life, the main thing that you need to survive. House or no house, I must have bread. Job or no job, I must have bread. We can take all the other stuff on the table and send it back with the waiter, and just put the "bread" right in the center. That is the important thing—everything else is extra. The Bread of Life is the most important thing in your home, in your family, in your marriage, in your life. I believe we are to diligently pursue the dreams God gives us, but we must never allow that pursuit to eclipse Jesus at the center.

> For what profit is it to a man if he gains the whole world, and loses his own soul?
>
> —MATTHEW 16:26

Fasting makes you hungry for what really matters in life. You realize that nothing else will satisfy. If that is not true in your life, then it is time to fast and pray until that hunger arises. One of the biggest problems in the church today is that we are so full on everything that the world has to offer that we have nothing to offer a starving world.

As a pastor, I want bread in every service. I don't preach well unless my mouth is full of bread. Our choir and praise team do not sing well unless their mouths are full of bread. There isn't a musician alive who can play well enough to set captives free unless breadcrumbs are falling off his fingers as he plays. They should only be up there full of the Bread of Life. We have many talented people in the church. But greater than talent is the bread.

Even if someone can't sing that well or preach that well, if they have been with Jesus, then they have what it takes to touch hearts and change lives! We must get the confusion out of the body of Christ: it's not about having church, or singing, or buildings, or budgets. It's not about religious "stuff." It's all about Jesus. When we get that part right, everything else will follow.

When the Bread of Life is present and that fresh aroma begins to fill the room, people do not want to leave. Paul and Silas were thrown into the inner part of a Roman prison with their feet shackled in chains. But instead of murmuring and complaining filling their mouths, their mouths were full of bread! They were singing and worshiping the Lord even at midnight, and the other inmates were listening. Then an earthquake shook the place and broke the chains of all who were bound, knocking the doors open as well.

The jailer, awakened by all the noise, thought all the prisoners had escaped and was about to kill himself when Paul assured him that they were all there. All of them. Not one prisoner left. Every crook, murderer, and thief remained. I believe the presence of God was so real in that place that not only did the jailer and his family get saved, but also prisoners who could get up and run chose to stay. That makes me think about Sunday mornings when people are meeting with God at the altars, getting free from addictions, coming to Jesus—while everyone else makes a mass exodus out of the back doors. I love to see times where, even though people can leave, they don't because they recognize the Bread of Life is in the room.

Are you the "breadwinner" in your home? Do you bring the Bread of Life into your home? When your children encounter difficult problems, do they come to you because you are the one with the Bread of Life? Do they see your walk with God daily, so that they will ask you about the Bible and expect you to give them spiritual answers? Do they see their parents fussing and arguing daily, or do they see you building each other up from the Word of God? Your home should be so filled with the Bread of Life that your children don't need to go elsewhere to get filled up.

> I want the Bread of Life more than anything else because everything else leaves me hungry.

On your eighteenth day of fasting, remember:

- Continue to journal your journey.

- Reflect on how this fast is causing you to grow spiritually.

- Allow your physical hunger to remind you to fill your spiritual hunger with Christ.

Thoughts for your journal:

- Is the Bread of Life the main course in your home, or has it been relegated to a side dish? Declare a fast today of everything in your home—television, video games, computers, cell phones, etc. that has taken the focus off of Jesus. Clear the table of everything and be filled again with the Bread of Life.

PRAYER FOCUS DAY 18: Satisfied With Nothing Else

As you continue to fast and pray, ask the Lord to fill you again. If Jesus Himself taught us to pray, "Give us this day our daily bread," then He promises there is something more of God that we can have today that we did not have yesterday. There will be something fresh tomorrow that today's bread just won't stretch to accommodate. Set your mind on the Bread of Life as your main dish and go after Him!

What things or people have replaced Christ as the main course in your life?

_____

_____

_____

> "Most assuredly, I say to you, Moses did not give you the bread from heaven, but My Father gives you the true bread from heaven. For the bread of God is He who comes down from heaven and gives life to the world." Then they said to Him, "Lord, give us this bread always." And Jesus said to them, "I am the bread of life. He who comes to Me shall never hunger, and he who believes in Me shall never thirst."
>
> —JOHN 6:32–35

In Acts 17, the Greeks were frantically looking for Paul and Silas to do them harm and throw them out of the city. When they couldn't find those two, they took a man named Jason, with whom Paul and Silas had stayed, and accused him of wrongdoing, saying, "These who have turned the world upside down have come here too" (v. 6). We will never turn the world upside down until the body of Christ consistently lives inside out. I am not impressed with how much people shout, how spiritual they act, or how big their Bibles may be. I want to know what is on the inside. That is who you really are. It is like the iceberg that sank the *Titanic*. Only about 20 percent of an iceberg is the part you can see above water. About 80 percent of an iceberg remains hidden under water. What is hidden in your private life matters to God. Your character—the person you are when no one else is looking—matters to God. Your integrity and purity matter to God. Who are you on the inside?

The longer I serve the Lord and the more I do what He has called me to do—the more I need to do a "gut check." Fasting is my gut check. I want to be open like David and look deep inside at the motives in my life. I want to ask myself, "Am I doing it for vainglory? Am I doing it because I'm an ambitious person?" Paul actually talked about missing the mark, about running only to find out that he lost the race.

> Do you not know that those who run in a race all run, but one receives the prize? Run in such a way that you may obtain it. And everyone who competes for the prize is temperate in all things. Now they do it to obtain a perishable crown, but we for an imperishable crown. Therefore I run thus: not with uncertainty. Thus I fight: not as one who beats the air. But I discipline my body and bring it into subjection, lest, when I have preached to others, I myself should become disqualified.
>
> —1 Corinthians 9:24–27

That is why I check myself on a regular basis by fasting regularly. Fasting is self-humbling! Fasting brings you to that place of saying, "Lord, create in me a clean heart. I want to bring You glory. I want to be a vessel You can use." I don't want to just be a preacher who gets up and presents a big, shiny front. I want something inside of me that connects with people. I don't want to talk to heads and tickle itching ears. I want to speak the piercing Word of God to hearts that need more of Jesus.

Coaches press athletes to dig deeper, yelling, "C'mon, boys; no guts, no glory!" They have to dig deep to overcome their opponents not only during the game but also in practice before the game. As a Christian the same rule applies. When you are not willing to get down into the "guts" of the matter, God is not willing to pour out His glory. He doesn't look on the exterior but on what is inside your heart.

I am tired of services where we just go through the motions and leave just as we came. We walk in neatly dressed and groomed, but we have all kinds of junk beneath the surface. We look like shiny balls of dirt! I believe that if we ever get clean on the inside and start living inside out, then God can release His glory upon His people. Are you ready for a purging? Are you ready for the cleansing of the fire of God? Do you want a fresh filling of His Spirit? Seek Him with prayer during this fast, and ask Him to search your innermost parts.

> If you allow sin to take root in your heart, when the Holy Spirit brings conviction about that sin the only cure is to be cleansed and changed from the inside out.

On your nineteenth day of fasting, remember:

- Make sure you are staying hydrated.

- Listen to your favorite worship music today.

- Don't grow weary! Stay strong in the power of His might.

Thoughts for your journal:

- When it comes to the heart of man, what goes in also comes out. What is on the inside will show on the outside. When you have junk inside—junk comes out. But in like manner, when you have Jesus inside—Jesus comes out. What do you think other people see coming out of you that reveals what is truly on the inside?

_____

_____

_____

PRAYER FOCUS DAY 19: A Clean Heart

As you pray today, consider the prayer that David prayed in Psalm 103 below. I believe David reached a point where he could bless the Lord with everything that was in him because he was not hiding anything from the eyes of God. His spirit was right. His heart was right. His conscience was clear. The question is, Can everything that is in you bless the Lord? Is your heart clean before Him today? Can you worship Him in spirit and in truth, or do you have "stuff" on the inside that does not bring glory to Him? The kind of worship God seeks can only come from deep within a clean heart.

What is God revealing to you today about the condition of your heart?

_____

_____

_____

_____

> Bless the LORD, O my soul; and all that
> is within me, bless His holy name!
>
> —PSALM 103:1

DAY 20: Winning the Real Battle

Y̶ou need to understand that the battle is not about what you're facing. The battle is not with your family or marriage, a financial problem, or an illness. The battle that must be won first is in your thinking. The devil desires to break down your mind. He wants to break you down mentally, to cause you to give up, to quit, to say, "I can't take it anymore. I'm going to use my quit option. I'm going to ring the bell and go back to how things used to be." You get to the point where you believe you have no more energy to fight and no ability to overcome. I'm here to remind you that you are more than conquerors in Christ Jesus, in His strength. But the only way that will become a reality in your life is if you remove the quit option. When you do that—the real battle is already won. The writer of the Book of Hebrews said:

> Therefore do not cast away your confidence, which has great reward. For you have need of endurance, so that after you have done the will of God, you may receive the promise.
>
> —Hebrews 10:35–36

We have need of endurance! Just as the Navy SEALs have to endure the grueling physical and mental strain in order to receive SEAL status, we need to endure the battles and overcome so that we may receive the promise of God. "We are not of those who draw back to perdition, but of those who believe to the saving of the soul" (Heb. 10:39). We do not draw back! I love that scripture because so many really do start out strong. They start out on fire for God, but somewhere along the way trouble starts breaking loose on every front. That's when they start looking for ways to draw back. It doesn't matter how strong you start if quitting is always an option.

I don't care what the enemy throws at me; I have made up my mind that I am not turning back. I am not of those who draw back, and I don't believe you are either. There is no quit option. I have had prayers answered, and I've had prayers go unanswered. I have had miracles happen, and I've endured huge disappointments. I've had high mountains where God gave me things and amazed me in awesome ways, and I've had low, low valleys where I felt God-forsaken and cried all night long. But I am not in this for what I can get out of Jesus. I'm in this because He loved me first and gave Himself for me. When I will recognize my weakness and trust in His strength, He will give me the mercy and grace to endure. "Let us therefore come boldly to the throne of grace, that we may obtain mercy and find grace to help in time of need" (Heb. 4:16).

However—and this is important—if the Lord were to never answer another prayer, I will *still* never quit. As Job said, "Though He slay me, yet will I trust Him" (Job 13:15). Job had thrown away the quit option. The three friends of Daniel—Shadrach, Meshach, and Abed-Nego—had thrown away the quit option. They told King Nebuchadnezzar:

> Our God whom we serve is able to deliver us from the burning fiery furnace, and He will deliver us from your hand, O king. But if not, let it be known to you, O king, that we do not serve your gods, nor will we worship the gold image which you have set up.
>
> —Daniel 3:17–18

They maintained their confidence in God's ability to deliver them, and even more, they had eliminated the quit option. Even if God *didn't* choose to deliver them from the fiery furnace, they would still not bow the knee to Nebuchadnezzar's idols.

> Fasting gives you the opportunity to come away from the bombardment of life's difficulties and disappointments in order to hear more clearly from the Lord.

On your twentieth day of fasting, remember:

- Pray and stay in God's Word.

- Worship God through music and praise.

- Cravings are apparent, but you've lasted this long!

Thoughts for your journal:

- How has this fast caused you to dig deeper in your walk with God?

- Have you sensed a new strength rising up within you as His Spirit fills you with fresh anointing?

_____

_____

_____

_____

DAY 20

PRAYER FOCUS DAY 20: No Turning Back

The number one thing the enemy would like us to do is quit. It may be quitting your marriage, quitting your dream, or even quitting your walk with the Lord. You could decide to quit battling your flesh through this fast and just give in to temptation even as you approach the final twenty-four hours. The devil is always filling your head with thoughts to make you give up, but when you set your mind on Christ and His example, you will not quit because Jesus never quit. Pray as Jesus did in the garden when He faced the greatest ordeal of His life. He could have said, "It's too much." He could have called legions of angels to defend Him. Yet He pressed on. Like Jesus, today you can pray for God's strength as you determine to do His will, not your own.

Write a declaration of your determination to finish whatever area of your life you've been tempted to quit:

_____

_____

_____

> Then Jesus said to His disciples, "If anyone
> wishes to come after Me, he must deny himself,
> and take up his cross and follow Me."
>
> —Matthew 16:24, nas

Sometimes the thing that prevents God from having His way in our lives is simply what is locked between our ears. Just as we do with old wardrobes, we tend to hold on to old ways of thinking, old patterns, old failures. The enemy convinces us that we will never be free of that thing we've been struggling with, that we are too weak to overcome it. When we stop trying to do things in our own power and instead choose to humble ourselves before God and trust Him to make over our weaknesses, the lies of the enemy lose their power! As the apostle Paul said:

> I beseech you therefore, brethren, by the mercies of God, that you present your bodies a living sacrifice, holy, acceptable to God, which is your reasonable service. And do not be conformed to this world, but be transformed by the renewing of your mind, that you may prove what is that good and acceptable and perfect will of God.
>
> —ROMANS 12:1–2

What if you could select a greater level of faith the same way you select a new nose or a new chin at the plastic surgeon's office? You could point to the faith of Joshua, who led the people of Israel into the Promised Land, saw the walls of Jericho fall according to God's instruction, and even commanded the sun to stand still so he could finish a battle one day. You could point to Peter's anointing for healing the sick with nothing but the passing of his shadow and say, "Lord, I desire an anointing like that." Or you could go for the ultimate package and say, "I want to be like Jesus."

I want you to understand that you should desire greater faith and greater anointing. Paul said we should "earnestly desire the best gifts" (1 Cor. 12:31). There's just one thing to keep in mind: there are no shortcuts. By now you've learned that. Fasting is not a requirement; it is a choice. You've chosen to complete this fast as a vow you made to pursue God on a deeper level. The entire time you've been on this fast, you were acknowledging God. When you felt hungry, empty, and weak, you connected with God without all the clutter. In that way this fast has strengthened your character in every area of your life. A lengthy fast strengthens your will. It strengthens your inner man. Like sharpening your ax for the work or battle of life, it helps you live in purity and holiness before God. Fasting helps you discipline your body to glorify God.

Fasting allowed you to lay your life on the master surgeon's table to have all the negative, deadly things cut away. He has replaced them with healthy, beautiful, life-giving characteristics. It took time, but you did not quit. You continued to trust God and He has honored the power of persistence in fasting and prayer. Now...enjoy the benefits of your extreme makeover!

> What concerns me is the number of Christians who would put faith in the process of a home makeover or even a physical makeover— but still not take the time to fast and pray, allowing the Lord to give them His makeover.

On your twenty-first day of fasting, remember:

- Share your experience of fasting with someone.

- Prepare to ease back into solid foods tomorrow, starting with soups and soft foods before you return to full meals.

- Be thankful and rejoice.

Thoughts for your journal:

- Praise God! Prepare for blessing, harvest, and an anointing like you have never experienced before.

- Get ready, because the rest of this year will not be like any other before it!

PRAYER FOCUS DAY 21: Bring It All to Him

Don't ever hesitate to show God your problem. As you come before Him on this final day of fasting, give Him every last withered part of your life. Hold nothing back. Give Him every hurt, every wounded area that hasn't healed yet…give Him your temper, your unforgiveness, things you didn't even know were affecting you—and trust Him to get to the root of those things and bring healing to those areas. When you bring your scars and issues to Him, He will give you a makeover, giving you beauty for ashes, strength for scars, and His grace to cover your weakness. Allow Him to give you an extreme makeover so you can walk in total freedom.

What things has the Holy Spirit brought to light on this final day of fasting?

_____

_____

_____

_____

_____

Therefore we also, since we are surrounded by so great a cloud of witnesses, let us lay aside every weight, and the sin which so easily ensnares us, and let us run with endurance the race that is set before us, looking unto Jesus, the author and finisher of our faith, who for the joy that was set before Him endured the cross, despising the shame, and has sat down at the right hand of the throne of God.

—Hebrews 12:1–2

Congratulations, you have endured! You did not quit! And you will never be the same!

Now, as you come out of your fast, be careful and ease back into eating solid foods over the next few days to a week. You must give your body time to recover and get used to digesting food again. Even though cravings may be strong in the first few days after the fast, pace yourself, and continue drinking plenty of fluids.

Maintaining the Fasting Edge

I trust that this time of fasting not only gave you back your edge, but it also took you to a whole new level in God. As you start back into "normal" life, determine that you won't live "normally" anymore! Do whatever it takes to maintain the fasting edge. Don't let the enemy regain any ground he lost during your fast.

There is no quit option in my emergency plan, and there should not be one in yours either. I have nothing to go back to. My worst day with Jesus is better than my best day in the world without God! I crossed that bridge a long time ago. The enemy, this world, difficult circumstances—it doesn't matter. I'll still be in church. I'll still lift my hands in worship. I'll still worship Him with my tithe. I'll still serve Him with all I have. I do not have a quit option in my mind anymore. Thank You, Lord, for the power of a made-up mind!

As I shared on Day 20, I am never going to quit. I am never going to walk away from God. I am never going to stop attending church. I am never going to leave my wife. I am never going to give up on my kids. I am never going to let my dream die. I am never going to quit preaching.

I am never going to quit living for Jesus. This needs to get deep in your spirit.

While preaching in Corinth, Paul went into a detailed discourse of some of the things he had encountered and endured after coming to Jesus. He had served the Lord with tears, in chains, against temptations and false accusations, and evading those who wanted him dead:

> …in labors more abundant, in stripes above measure, in prisons more frequently, in deaths often. From the Jews five times I received forty stripes minus one. Three times I was beaten with rods; once I was stoned; three times I was shipwrecked; a night and a day I have been in the deep; in journeys often, in perils of waters, in perils of robbers, in perils of my own countrymen, in perils of the Gentiles, in perils in the city, in perils in the wilderness, in perils in the sea, in perils among false brethren; in weariness and toil, in sleeplessness often, in hunger and thirst, in fastings often, in cold and nakedness—besides the other things, what comes upon me daily: my deep concern for all the churches.
>
> —2 CORINTHIANS 11:23–28

Paul had a made-up mind that he would not only finish the race, but also that he was going to do it with joy! There was no quit option for him. He was bombarded with trials and attacks everywhere he went, but that did not change his resolve, and we cannot allow it to change ours either. If anything, it should make us stronger. As Paul said, "Yet in all these things we are more than conquerors through Him who loved us. For I am persuaded that neither death nor life, nor angels nor principalities nor powers, nor things present nor things to come, nor height nor depth, nor any other created thing, shall be able to separate us from the love of God which is in Christ Jesus our Lord" (Rom. 8:37–39).

Jesus is our ultimate example. He is the "author and finisher of our faith" (Heb. 12:2). He endured from beginning to end. He never took short-cuts. He never quit. He endured the whip when they beat His back until it looked like ribbons falling from His flesh. He endured the beating, the humiliation, the spit, the accusations, and the soldier's slaps across His face. He endured the nails as they stretched Him across the timbers of the cross and brutally pierced His hands and His feet. He could have quit—but He endured. He was set from the beginning to carry out the will of the Father and redeem fallen man—you and me—no matter what. If He can do that, He can bring you through anything!

BENEFITS OF CORPORATE FASTING

I n this journal you've read that fasting connects you to your assignment and accelerates your destiny. I believe the promise of fasting not only changes your own destiny but coming together to participate in corporate (group) fasting can also change the destinies of your community and your nation. If you've never participated in a corporate fast, I want to challenge you to consider the worldwide impact this type of fasting can have. In the Bible there are two cases in particular where corporate fasting literally changed history!

Nineveh Finds Favor

According to Scripture, Nineveh was in trouble. This city, which was full of wickedness, was headed for destruction (Jon. 3:4)…but they were not without hope. When Jonah took this message of impending destruction to Nineveh, the people took God seriously. Their only hope was to cry out to God through prayer and fasting. And that is exactly what they did.

> So the people of Nineveh believed God, proclaimed a fast, and put on sackcloth, from the greatest to the least of them.
> —JONAH 3:5

As a nation they repented before God and fasted. This is what the king of Nineveh decreed: "Let neither man nor beast, herd nor flock, taste anything; do not let them eat, or drink water.…Who can tell if God will turn and relent, and turn away from His fierce anger, so that we may not perish?" (Jon. 3:7, 9). And it worked!

Then God saw their works, that they turned from their evil way; and God relented from the disaster that He had said He would bring upon them, and He did not do it.

—Jonah 3:10

The people of Nineveh actually changed God's mind through prayer and fasting! This corporate fast released God's mercy and changed history. Without the fast of repentance, would Nineveh have survived? Absolutely not! We also know that Nineveh was not judged for another two hundred years after that.

Seventy-Two Hours That Saved the Jews

Another time when fasting changed history for a nation is found in the Book of Esther. The Jews were on the verge of destruction because of the evil conspiracy of Haman, one of the king's advisors. Haman was "filled with wrath" against a Jew named Mordecai because he "did not bow or pay him homage" (Esther 3:5).

Mordecai sought help from Queen Esther, who was his cousin. Mordecai's request meant Esther would have to literally risk her life—for it was very dangerous for her to approach the king without being summoned first. So Esther called a fast.

Go, gather all the Jews who are present in Shushan, and fast for me; neither eat nor drink for three days, night or day. My maids and I will fast likewise. And so I will go to the king, which is against the law; and if I perish, I perish!

—Esther 4:16

Those seventy-two hours of fasting changed the history of the world. When Esther approached the king on behalf of her people, they became a nation not of defeat, annihilation, suffering, and shame, but a nation of favor. They received honor and promotion...all because of three days of fasting and prayer.

You and I can help change the history of our own nation through prayer and fasting. Yes, we have become a world void of morality and truth. But we don't have to accept it! I want to challenge you to make a habit of regular prayer and fasting for our nation. Fast and pray for our leaders. Fast and pray for our religious freedoms. Fast and pray for the multitudes who have been deceived by the enemy.

When the economy is in trouble...when we are worried about wars and hostile nations...when natural disasters take homes and lives, we are to call a solemn assembly and fast. We are the ambassadors of Christ, and we can affect change.

In the Book of Joel God promises a latter-day outpouring of His Spirit.

> And it shall come to pass afterward that I will pour out My Spirit on all flesh; your sons and daughters shall prophesy, your old men shall dream dreams, your young men shall see visions. And also on My menservants and on My maidservants I will pour out My Spirit in those days.
>
> —Joel 2:28–29

But this great End Time outpouring can only come through prayer and fasting. Joel 1:14 says, "Consecrate a fast, call a sacred assembly; gather the elders and all the inhabitants of the land into the house of the Lord your God, and cry out to the Lord." Will you join God's people in crying out for His Spirit? Just like the fasting and prayers of the people of Nineveh and Esther and her people, your fasting and prayers can change history!

THE BENEFITS OF A FASTED LIFESTYLE

You may have concluded this twenty-one-day fast, but I challenge you to consider making fasting a part of your lifestyle from now on. As you do, keep in mind that your sacrifice can have a worldwide effect. The following tips can help you strategize for ways to make fasting a part of your lifestyle.

Ways You Can Make Fasting a Part of Your Lifestyle

• Schedule a day each month to fast throughout the year. You may want to fast the first day of each month…the first Sunday of the month…or lunch every other Wednesday.

• Give up certain foods for one week as a fast, like cookies or caffeinated drinks.

• Find a "fasting partner" at work or in your community and meet for prayer and Bible study during lunch once a week or once a month.

• Along with fasting food, go on a "TV fast" with your family. Fast television at specific times throughout the year. It could be for a week or one day a month. When you do, use that time for family prayer and Bible study. You'll be amazed at all the time you have for reading, homework, games, and more!

- Select a few dates throughout the year that you and your spouse can have a "date fast." Instead of going out to eat, get a babysitter and find a private place to go with your spouse for a special time of prayer over your family.

- Fast on special dates throughout the year. Fast for your family and loved ones on their birthdays, anniversaries, or other dates that are important to your family.

- You can probably think of other fasting times that would be personal for you and your family.

Fasting Scripture Reference Guide

Blessings of fasting
Deuteronomy 28:2, 13–14;
2 Chronicles 7:14; Isaiah 58:8

Corporate fasting
1 Samuel 7:5–6; 2 Chronicles
30–34; Ezra 8:21–23;
Nehemiah 9:1–3; Joel
2:15–16; Jonah 3:5–10; Acts
27:33–37

Daniel fast
Daniel 10:2–3

Esther fast
Esther 4:16

Fasting dos
Matthew 6:16–18

Fasting don'ts
Matthew 6:16–18; Luke
18:9–14

Prayer and Scripture go
with fasting
1 Samuel 1:6–8; Nehemiah
1:4; Daniel 9:3, 20; Joel 2:12;
Luke 2:37; Acts 10:30; 13:2; 1
Corinthians 7:5

Preparing to fast
Mark 11:25; Luke 11:4;
Romans 12:1–2

When to fast
Matthew 9:14–15

Why fast
1 Samuel 7:3; Isaiah 58:6;
Matthew 6:33; Mark 9:29;
Luke 4:1–13; Romans 12:1

A Forty-Day Strategy for Triumph

Now that you've completed a twenty-one-day fast, you may be wondering about extending your fasting experience even longer next time. Here's a quick strategy that will help you embark on a forty-day fast that produces great results in your life.

The Lord of the Flies

One of the biblical names for Satan is "Beelzebub," which means "lord of the flies." In the Bible, flies and pests are representative of demon spirits. Demon spirits such as generational curses, bondages, and strongholds of the mind can attach themselves to our lives, persistently buzzing around in our heads like irritating flies. We swat them, but they just keep coming back.

Are you tormented by certain "flies" or recurring problems and temptations in your life? If you want the victory once and for all, the Lord has given you a strategy for triumph—fasting. If you will consecrate a period of time for special sacrifice and intimacy with the Lord, you will experience deliverance from "flies" you've tried to get rid of for years.

Eradicate the Flies

Scientists have discovered something interesting about killing flies. To completely eradicate them, you must spray insecticides for a period of forty days because that is the length of a fly's reproductive cycle. If you spray consistently over a forty-day cycle, you will not only kill the present flies but will also wipe out future generations.

In the same way you can eliminate evil spirits from your life and your children's lives with a season of consecrated, continual prayer. Satan is a short-term skirmisher. Demons cannot stand the power of the Holy Ghost and intimate presence of Jesus that happens when you pray and fast.

Fasting That Produces Results

While I do believe there's something significant about a forty-day fast, the Bible records many different circumstances, types, and lengths of fasts, many of which I've shared with you in my various books on fasting. Don't be discouraged if you think you cannot fast for forty days. Don't bite off more than you can handle. There's no need to be heroic and attempt a forty-day fast if you've never fasted a day in your life. Just start. Once you discover the benefits, you'll be on your way to making it a life practice.

This journal guided you through a twenty-one-day fast. Daniel partially fasted for twenty-one days and often fasted one day at a time. The results of his twenty-one-day fast in which he only abstained from breads and meat and drank only water were powerful enough in the spirit realm to get the attention of the archangel Michael (Dan. 10:2–3). It's recorded that the apostle Paul was on at least two fasts, one for three days and one for fourteen days. Peter fasted for three days; Judah, Ezra, the people of Nineveh, Nehemiah, David, and Anna are also among those whose fasts are noted in the Word. Whatever time you are able to set aside and consecrate to God is more than worth it. God will honor the sacrifice made in His name.

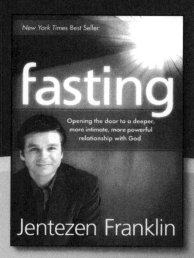